MW00986846

The Battle of Antietam

Books in the Battles Series:

The Attack on Pearl Harbor
The Battle of Antietam
The Battle of Belleau Wood
The Battle of Britain
The Battle of Gettysburg
The Battle of Hastings
The Battle of Marathon
The Battle of Midway

The Battle of Stalingrad
The Battle of Waterloo
The Battle of Zama
The Charge of the Light Brigade
Defeat of the Spanish Armada
The Inchon Invasion
The Invasion of Normandy
The Tet Offensive

✷ Battles of the Civil War ✷

The Battle of Antietam

by James P. Reger

Lucent Books, P.O. Box 289011, San Diego, CA 92198-9011

Library of Congress Cataloging-in-Publication Data

Reger, James P.
    The Battle of Antietam / by James P. Reger
        p. cm. — (Battles of the Civil War)
    Includes bibliographical references and index.
    Summary: Examines the events preceding, during, and after the
Battle of Antietam in 1862.
    ISBN 1-56006-454-4 (alk. paper)
    1. Antietam, Battle of, Md., 1862—Juvenile literature.
[1. Antietam, Battle of, Md., 1862. 2. United States—History—
Civil War, 1861–1865—Campaigns.] I. Title. II. Series.
E474.65.R44 1997
973.7'336—dc20
                                                        96-14415
                                                          CIP
                                                           AC

Printed in the U.S.A.

Contents

Foreword

Almost everyone would agree with William Tecumseh Sherman that war "is all hell." Yet the history of war, and battles in particular, is so fraught with the full spectrum of human emotion and action that it becomes a microcosm of the human experience. Soldiers' lives are condensed and crystallized in a single battle. As Francis Miller explains in his *Photographic History of the Civil War* when describing the war wounded, "It is sudden, the transition from marching bravely at morning on two sound legs, grasping your rifle in two sturdy arms, to lying at nightfall under a tree with a member forever gone."

Decisions made on the battlefield can mean the lives of thousands. A general's pique or indigestion can result in the difference between life and death. Some historians speculate, for example, that Napoleon's fateful defeat at Waterloo was due to the beginnings of stomach cancer. His stomach pain may have been the reason that the normally decisive general was sluggish and reluctant to move his troops. And what kept George McClellan from winning battles during the Civil War? Some scholars and contemporaries believe that it was simple cowardice and fear. Others argue that he felt a gut-wrenching unwillingness to engage in the war of attrition that was characteristic of that particular conflict.

Battle decisions can be magnificently brilliant and horribly costly. At the Battle of Thaspus in 47 B.C., for example, Julius Caesar, facing a numerically superior army, shrewdly ordered his troops onto a narrow strip of land bordering the sea. Just as he expected, his enemy thought he had accidentally trapped himself and divided their forces to surround his troops. By dividing their army, his enemy had given Caesar the strategic edge he needed to defeat them. Other battle orders result in disaster, as in the case of the Battle at Balaklava during the Crimean War in 1854. A British general gave the order to attack a force of withdrawing enemy Russians. But confusion in relaying the order resulted in the 670 men of the Light Brigade's charging in the wrong direction into certain death by heavy enemy cannon fire. Battles are the stuff of history on the grandest scale—their outcomes often determine whether nations are enslaved or liberated.

Moments in battles illustrate the best and worst of human character. In the feeling of terror and the us-versus-them attitude that accompanies war, the enemy can be dehumanized and treated with a contempt that is considered repellent in times of peace. At Wounded Knee, the distrust and anticipation of violence that grew between the Native Americans and American soldiers led to the senseless killing of ninety men, women, and children. And who can forget My Lai, where the deaths of old men, women, and children at the hands of American soldiers shocked an America already disillusioned with the Vietnam War. The murder of six million Jews will remain burned into the human conscience forever as the measure of man's inhumanity to man. These horrors cannot be forgotten. And yet, under the terrible conditions of battle, one can find acts of bravery, kindness, and altruism. During the Battle of Midway, the members of Torpedo Squadron 8, flying in hopelessly antiquated planes and without the benefit of air protection from fighters, tried bravely to fulfill their mission—to destroy the *Kido Butai,* the Japanese Carrier Striking Force. Without air support, the squadron was immediately set upon by Japanese fighters. Nevertheless, each bomber tried valiantly to hit his target. Each failed. Every man but one died in the effort. But by keeping the Japanese fighters busy, the squadron bought time and delayed further Japanese fighter attacks. In the aftermath of the Battle of Isandhlwana in South Africa in 1879, a force of thousands of Zulu warriors trapped a contingent of British troops in a small trading post. After repeated bloody attacks in which many died on both sides, the Zulus, their final victory certain, granted the remaining British their lives as a gesture of respect for their bravery. During World War I, American troops were so touched by the fate of French war orphans that they took up a collection to help them. During the Civil War, soldiers of the North and South would briefly forget that they were enemies and share smokes and coffee across battle lines during the endless nights. These acts seem all the more dramatic, more uplifting, because they indicate that people can continue to behave with humanity when faced with inhumanity.

Lucent Books' Battles Series highlights the vast range of the human character revealed in the ordeal of war. Dramatic narrative describes in exciting and accurate detail the commanders, soldiers, weapons, strategies, and maneuvers involved in each battle. Each volume includes a comprehensive historical context, explaining what brought the parties to war, the events leading to the battle, what factors made the battle important, and the effects it had on the larger war and later events.

The Battles Series also includes a chronology of important dates that gives students an overview, at a glance, of each battle. Sidebars create a broader context by adding enlightening details on leaders, institutions, customs, warships, weapons, and armor mentioned in the narration. Every volume contains numerous maps that allow readers to better visualize troop movements and strategies. In addition, numerous primary and secondary source quotations drawn from both past historical witnesses and modern historians are included. These quotations demonstrate to readers how and where historians derive information about past events. Finally, the volumes in the Battles Series provide a launching point for further reading and research. Each book contains a bibliography designed for student research, as well as a second bibliography that includes the works the author consulted while compiling the book.

Above all, the Battles Series helps illustrate the words of Herodotus, the fifth-century B.C. Greek historian now known as the "father of history." In the opening lines of his great chronicle of the Greek and Persian Wars, the world's first battle book, he set for himself this goal: "To preserve the memory of the past by putting on record the astonishing achievements both of our own and of other peoples; and more particularly, to show how they came into conflict."

Chronology of Events

August 29–30 Confederates rout Federals at Second Battle of Bull Run (Manassas) in northern Virginia.

Monday, September 1 Federals fight off rearguard attack by Confederates at Chantilly, Virginia.

September 1–6 Union forces retreat toward Washington.

Tuesday, September 2 President Lincoln reinstates George B. McClellan as commander of the Army of the Potomac.

Wednesday, September 3 General Robert E. Lee's Army of Northern Virginia begins marching toward the Potomac River crossings and Maryland beyond.

September 4–6 Lee's men cross the Potomac; the invasion of Maryland begins.

Saturday, September 6 The Rebels reach Frederick, Maryland.

Sunday, September 7 McClellan starts his army northward from the Rockville, Maryland (Washington) area.

Monday, September 8 Lee issues proclamation to the people of Maryland encouraging them to rise up with him in rebellion; very few do.

Tuesday, September 9 Lee issues Special Orders No. 191 calling for a division of his army and the capture of Harpers Ferry; McClellan slowly moves a few more miles to the north, advancing on three roads.

Wednesday, September 10 The Confederate Army of Northern Virginia leaves Frederick, heading west toward South Mountain.

Thursday, September 11 Lee crosses South Mountain; Jackson and two separate columns approach Harpers Ferry from different directions; McClellan continues his cautious advance; Lee further divides his men and sends Longstreet north with this fourth force toward Hagerstown to meet a rumored threat there.

Friday, September 12 Cavalry skirmishes continue; the first Yankees charge into Frederick, chasing out the rearguard Confederates; the divided Confederate forces tighten the ring around Harpers Ferry.

Saturday, September 13 McClellan and the main body of the Union army receive a hero's welcome as they enter Frederick; the vanguard of the Union army arrives east of South Mountain for an attack the next day.

Sunday, September 14 The Battle of South Mountain.

Monday, September 15 With less than half of his army reconstituted, Lee takes up positions on the heights overlooking Antietam Creek; Jackson captures Harpers Ferry; McClellan and his army arrive in the Antietam Valley but do not attack.

Tuesday, September 16 Both armies prepare for battle and bring up additional forces; McClellan holds a 2-to-1 advantage in manpower (80,000 Union versus 40,000 Confederates) but he cautiously postpones his attack until the next day.

Wednesday, September 17, 1862: The Battle of Antietam

6:00 A.M. to 9:00 A.M. Miller's cornfield on the north end of the battlefield. Union general Joseph Hooker and Confederate general Thomas J. "Stonewall" Jackson fight to a bloody draw; the field changes hands thirteen times.

9:00 A.M. to 10:00 A.M. The West Woods. Union general Edwin Sumner leads his men into what amounts to a trap; In a dense patch of forest, his men are nearly wiped out by hidden Confederates under Jackson; the fighting in the north subsides; McClellan refuses to send in reserves which surely would have won him the battle.

10:00 A.M. to 12:00 P.M. Bloody Lane. In the middle of the battlefield, D. H. Hill's Confederates turn an old farm lane into a trench and fend off three Union attacks before their line bursts wide open; again, McClellan commits no reserves to exploit his advantage.

11:00 A.M. to 1:00 P.M. Burnside's Bridge. On the south end of the battlefield, Union general Ambrose Burnside hesitates to attack with his entire force; as a result, Confederate general Robert Toombs and a handful of Rebel sharpshooters prevent the Yankees from crossing the creek; Burnside finally commits enough strength to take the bridge but not before wasting two hours.

3:00 P.M. to 3:40 P.M. Sharpsburg Ridge. After delaying another two hours, Burnside sends his force up the hill to mop up Lee's remnants outside the village; unable to hold the Federals back any longer, the Confederates begin to break and run; all appears lost for the Rebels until General A. P. Hill arrives from Harpers Ferry in the nick of time with the last division of Confederate reinforcements.

3:40 P.M. to 5:00 P.M. The slopes leading back down to the bridge. A. P. Hill's troops smash into the Union flank; in a fighting retreat, the Federals fall back to their positions at Burnside's Bridge.

5:00 P.M. to 6:00 P.M. The entire Antietam battlefield. The battle sounds finally wind down and are replaced by the moans of 16,000 wounded men; the sun sets on the bloodiest single day in American history.

INTRODUCTION

The Rising Southern Tide

On Thursday, September 4, 1862, the forty-thousand men and boys of General Robert E. Lee's Army of Northern Virginia arose at dawn and secured their gear on their bodies for the noisy tramp into Union-held Maryland. The suntanned soldiers looked like one-man bands with their dangling pots, pans, canteens, and bayonets. The racket they made as they shuffled into the yellow dust was every bit as disconcerting to northern spectators as the sight of the grimy Rebel troops.

One Marylander said, "They [the Confederate soldiers] were the dirtiest men I ever saw, a most ragged and hungry set of wolves." Another added that, in spite of their shabby appearance, "there was a dash about them that the Northern men lacked."

Marching four abreast to the rhythms of brass bands, this muddy river of gaunt, unkempt men filled the narrow road for miles in either direction. Their nonuniform clothing (dissimilar due to the Confederate army's lack of money and supplies) tumbled together browns, grays, blacks, and reds. Their weapons were as individual as their clothing. But one thing about them remained consistent: the confidence they exuded in their ultimate victory over the North.

Although Northerners scoffed at the shabby, disparate uniforms of the Confederate soldiers, they could not discount the Rebels' accomplishments in battle.

In South Carolina, Confederates reduced the once mighty Union stronghold Fort Sumter to ruins.

It was easy to understand why the Confederates were so confident. They had won nearly every battle of the war thus far, starting with the battle at Fort Sumter in Charleston, South Carolina, during which they blasted that mighty island fortress into rubble. The First Battle of Manassas came three months later, and the Confederates routed the Yankees in northern Virginia, chasing them all the way back to Washington.

During the Shenandoah Valley campaign that followed First Manassas, Stonewall Jackson defeated three separate Union armies. Next General Robert E. Lee and his Southerners won the Seven Days' Battles on the Peninsula east of Richmond. They managed to drive General George B. McClellan's huge Union force back into the Chesapeake Bay. Their recent victory at the Second Battle of Manassas and now their sudden thrust into Maryland had raised Confederate hopes to an even greater peak. Scratching their lice and ignoring their hunger, the Confederate soldiers pressed on with the fire of conquest in their eyes.

Now the soldiers were taking the next step in their winning strategy. Lee's plan was to wear down the North, making the public tired of war. Lee hoped that Maryland, with its many Southern sympathizers, might be freed of Union occupation forces and encouraged to join the Confederacy. This strategy would allow the Confederates to surround the United States capital, which was located between the states of Maryland and Virginia. Once these gains were realized, the Confederates hoped that much needed English support would be forthcoming and that the crumbling morale of the Union forces would likely collapse altogether.

From Despair to Hope

Indeed, twenty-five miles to the south, the mangled remains of the Union army just defeated at Second Manassas were trudging back to Washington. One historian said that they "had been kicked, cuffed, hustled about, knocked down, run over, and trodden upon as rarely happens in the history of war." A Union colonel who witnessed the retreat remarked, "There was everywhere along the road the greatest confusion. Infantry, cavalry,

Stonewall Jackson surveys the battlefield during the First Battle of Manassas. His Confederate troops vanquished the Union army here, forcing the defeated Yankees to withdraw from northern Virginia.

artillery and wagons all hurried on pell mell in the midst of the futile rallying cries of officers."

The Northern soldiers talked little except to complain about their incompetent commander, John Pope. The bombastic general had achieved a few moderate successes along the Mississippi River, and in his first order to these eastern soldiers, he had pompously decried:

> I have come to you from the West where we have always seen the backs of our enemies. Dismiss from your minds certain phrases which I am sorry to find much in vogue amongst you. I hear constantly of "taking strong positions and holding them," of "lines of retreat and bases of supplies." Let us discard such ideas. Let us look before and not behind. Success and glory are in the advance!

(Top) Despite the Union losses at the First Battle of Manassas, General George McClellan was able to inspire the discouraged Yankees and transform them into fierce soldiers. John Pope (pictured), the commander of the doomed Second Manassas campaign, was not so fortunate and was considered incompetent by his troops.

When he loudly proclaimed, "My headquarters will be in my saddle," the joke began that he did not know his headquarters from his hindquarters.

No one was joking now though, least of all General Pope. He was just slouching in his saddle-headquarters and drearily plodding back toward Washington. The spirits of the men picked up, however, when an excited officer rode up and cried, "Boys! McClellan is in command of the Army again! Three cheers!" The cheers erupted at the beginning of the column and waved fifteen miles back to the end.

The reason was simple. These men loved Little Mac in spite of his lusterless battle record. He had picked them up and brushed them off after their humiliating defeat a year earlier at the First Battle of Manassas. He had molded them into a self-respecting fighting force and inspired them with parades and reviews. Masterfully, the Little Napoleon had convinced them that this war was worth dying in even though very few of them really knew what it was all about.

CHAPTER ONE

Causes, Stakes, and Odds

Slavery in the United States probably began in the murky shadows of pre-history. Certainly, Native Americans practiced slavery among themselves long before the advent of the first European colonies. Spain, Portugal, France, and England were the first to bring slaves from Africa for purposes of forced manual labor. These unfortunate Blacks began arriving in Jamestown, Virginia, in 1619 to work on the developing tobacco plantations.

Human bondage was so entrenched in America 169 years later that every man who signed the U.S. Constitution either owned slaves or believed that slavery could not be abolished by a central government. Thomas Jefferson said allowing slavery was like "holding a wolf by the ears. You did not like it but you did not dare let it go." He and the other Founding Fathers agreed to leave the decision regarding the issue of slave ownership to each state.

The Northern states (with neither plantations nor the need of slaves) eventually did prohibit the institution of slavery. But the Southern states, convinced of slavery's economic benefits, decided to retain the tradition. One Southern senator even saw slavery as a natural reflection of human progress, commenting: "There is not a respectable system of civilization known to history whose foundations were not laid in the institution of domestic slavery." He and others argued that slavery had Christianized the pagan Africans, saving their very souls from eternal damnation.

These differences in point of view made for a touchy problem when the vast western territories began to petition for statehood. If these incoming states continued to decide the slavery

issue for themselves, their choices would affect the balance of power in the Federal government. Too many slave or too many free states could result in political decisions being tipped to one side's advantage, and neither side wanted to risk being dominated by the other. So between 1820 and 1854, Congress passed a series of compromises in an attempt to maintain an equality of political power between the North and the South.

In the first such compromise, the House of Representatives voted to admit Maine into the Union as a free (nonslave) state. However, the addition would have made twelve free states as opposed to only eleven slave states, and the South was not about to allow the North to dominate. It took the bargaining skills of a hard-drinking, hard-gambling senator with a genius for solving political problems, the Honorable Henry Clay from Kentucky, to hammer out a bill acceptable to both the Northern and the Southern states. Maine would be allowed to join the Union, but the slave state of Missouri would be admitted at the same time. The year was 1820, and the bill became known as the Missouri Compromise.

(Top) Although slavery was common in the South, Northerners continued to call for its abolishment. In order to keep a balance of power between slave and free states, Kentucky senator Henry Clay (pictured) composed the Missouri Compromise.

Congress admitted Texas, a slave state, to the Union in 1845 without adding a corresponding free state. Instead, the Northerners accepted the promise that slavery would be prohibited from any other western lands that might be won or bought from Mexico. Accordingly, the Wilmot Proviso passed through Congress the following year with the clear guarantee that "neither slavery nor involuntary servitude shall ever exist in any part of the territories acquired from Mexico." Both sides were happy, but not for long. Within another year, the Southerners were questioning the constitutionality of the proviso, and sectional tensions were on the rise again.

California came into the Union in 1850 as a free state (balancing the ratio once again) without being paired with a slave state. To satisfy the South this time, the Wilmot Proviso was reversed, leaving open once again the question of whether to allow slavery in the other western territories. The Southerners also passed a Fugitive Slave Act that replaced one by Congress in 1793. The new law made it easier for owners to regain their runaway slaves. Almost as an afterthought, selling slaves (but not slavery itself) was banned in the nation's capital, Washington, D.C.

The final (and most disastrous) attempt at compromise came in 1854 when Senator Stephen A. Douglas introduced the Kansas-Nebraska Act. With it, he hoped to put into practice the theory called "popular sovereignty." Popular sovereignty called for the people living within a given territory to decide for themselves whether or not to allow slavery. When the provisions of the act became public, settlers for and against slavery began pouring into the two territories in order to promote their respective causes. Elections became shams. Violence followed.

That violence took the name "Bleeding Kansas" and for good reason. Throughout the remainder of the decade, slavers and free staters shot, hanged, and knifed each other until the murder count rose above fifty; still the slavery issue was not decided. A case in point: John Brown, the fiery abolitionist destined for both martyrdom and infamy, dragged five members of a proslavery family from their home in Pottawatomie Creek, Kansas, one night and hacked them into pieces while the victims' women and young children looked on. He was never prosecuted for the crime. The homes and belongings of many of those who escaped death were burned to ashes and whole families took to the road as refugees.

It was becoming clear that the congressional compromises were not working. Many Northerners were growing impatient with the sluggish political process and wanted to abolish slavery immediately. Some gave speeches calling for the prompt abolition of slavery, and others published newspapers emphasizing the immorality of slave ownership. A soft-spoken woman by the name of Harriet Beecher Stowe published *Uncle Tom's Cabin*, agitating the North with its horrifying depiction of Southerners and how they treated their slaves. The abolitionist author Henry

James said, "That triumphant work was much less a book than a state of vision."

Southerners viewed that "state of vision" and other similar writings as propaganda and proof that Northerners were not interested in compromises of any kind. They saw the Yankees' only purpose in their speeches and writings as inciting "servile insurrection." The threat of such slave rebellions had long haunted Southerners. In fact, there had already been several bloody revolts that had claimed the lives of Blacks and Whites alike. Compromise to slave owners meant inching ever closer to another such catastrophe, and they were becoming less and less willing to take the risk.

The strains between North and South nearly ruptured when the same John Brown of Kansas mounted a guerrilla operation that he hoped would inspire the slaves to rise up and free themselves (exactly as the Southerners feared). Intending to arm the Blacks with rifles stolen from the U.S. arsenal at Harpers Ferry,

Northerners John Brown (above, left) and Harriet Beecher Stowe (left) both worked to further the abolitionist movement, yet used extremely different measures; Brown resorted to violence whereas Stowe turned to writing.

Somewhere in the Middle

Abolitionists in the North and plantation owners in the South presented predictably different portraits of slavery. Each interpretation was calculated to either inflame or calm the sensibilities of those observers as yet undecided concerning the slavery issue. Through novels, plays, photographs, and paintings, both sides exaggerated the conditions in which the slaves lived in order to promote their particular point of view.

On one hand, Harriet Beecher Stowe's *Uncle Tom's Cabin* emphasized the cruelties of slavery and described the whippings and beatings slaves received. On the other hand, Stephen Foster wrote songs like "Old Black Joe" and "Massa's in de Cold, Cold Ground" that sentimentalized the "good life" of the slave.

Historians believe that the following words of a former field hand reflect average (not the best, not the worst) living conditions at the time. Readers may decide for themselves whether the abolitionist's or the plantation owner's portrait of slavery was the closest to the truth.

Our dress was of tow cloth and a pair of coarse shoes once a year. We lodged in log huts. Wooden floors were an unknown luxury. In a single room were huddled, like cattle, ten or a dozen persons, men, women, and children. There were neither bedsteads or furniture. Our beds were collections of straw and old rags. The wind whistled and the rain and snow blew in through the cracks, and the damp earth soaked in the moisture till the floor was miry as a pig-sty. But we slept good anyway because we were always so tired.

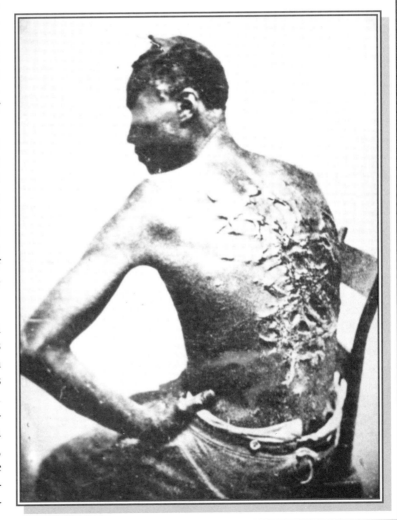

A former slave displays the hideous web of scars that resulted from repeated whippings and beatings. Abolitionists condemned plantation owners, asserting that all slaves endured these same cruelties.

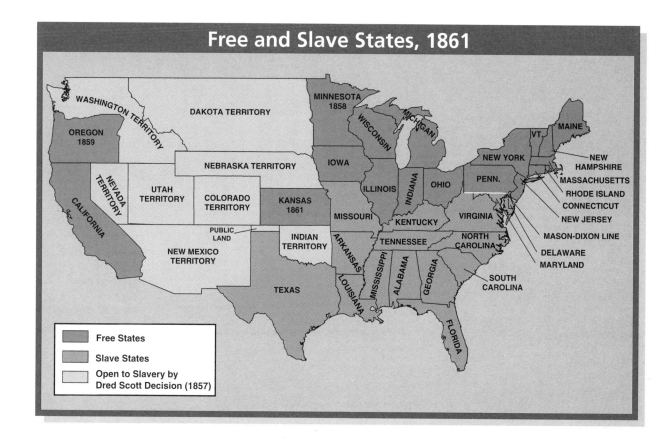

Free and Slave States, 1861

Free States

Slave States

Open to Slavery by
Dred Scott Decision (1857)

Virginia (now West Virginia), Brown and a small band of followers attacked the Federal gun works there.

Although the raid failed and Brown was hanged for treason, Southerners saw this direct appeal to the slaves as proof of a Northern conspiracy bent on inciting the slaves to revolt. Convinced that the Northerners wanted to dominate them politically and now by force of arms as well, the Southerners began to prepare for what they were already calling their "second war for independence." The talking was over. The compromises had failed. War was inevitable, and it would begin at Fort Sumter on April 12, 1861.

Pluses and Minuses: The Tally Sheet

By 1862 the Northern soldiers were holding every material advantage. They outnumbered the Southerners two to one. Some observers claimed the ratio was closer to three to one, and the reason was obvious. Twenty million people lived in the North. Although nine million lived in the South, a third of them were slaves whom the Confederates did not dare arm.

Population was not the only advantage that the Northern states possessed. Agriculturally, the North grew almost all the corn, wheat, and oats in America. In contrast, the Southern plantations specialized in cash crops, such as tobacco, indigo, and especially

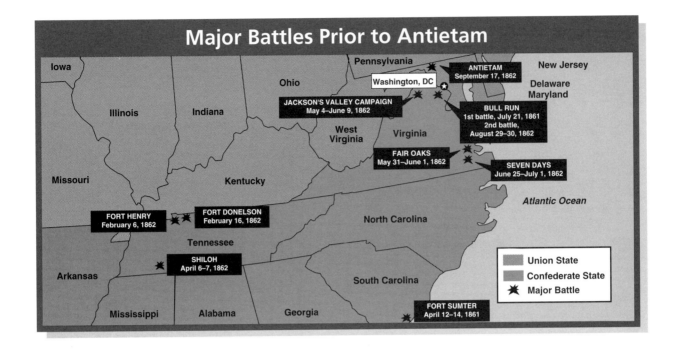

cotton, and the Federal naval blockade had limited their access to food crops from outside sources.

The Northerners were also more industrialized and had twice the number of railroads for moving men and supplies. In addition, they maintained many more miles of telegraph lines for communicating and could boast of ten times more factories than the South for producing guns, uniforms, and other war equipment. With all of these assets, Northern newspapermen and politicians were beginning to press for answers to some glaring questions. They wanted to know why the Union army had been losing battle after battle to the undermanned, underprovisioned Rebels.

And the questions were justified. During the eighteen months since their humiliation at Fort Sumter, the Federals had, indeed, lost most of the major battles despite their superiority in manpower and supplies. In 1861, they had "skedaddled" at First Bull Run, jumped in desperation from the deadly cliffs of Ball's Bluff, Virginia, and fled from repeated Southern attacks at Wilson's Creek, Missouri.

The first half of 1862 proved to be no less discouraging for the Unionists. In Virginia's Shenandoah Valley, they lost to "Stonewall" Jackson at McDowell, Front Royal, Winchester, Cross Keys, and Port Republic. On the Richmond peninsula, the Yankees added to their string of losses by surrendering the field to Robert E. Lee at Fair Oaks, Mechanicsville, Gaines' Mill, and Malvern Hill. They then retreated by ship all the way back to Washington in time to be defeated again by Lee and Jackson at Second Manassas.

After the Federal loss at Second Manassas, an influential Northerner wrote:

The nation is rapidly sinking just now. Stonewall Jackson (our national bugaboo) is about to invade Maryland, 40,000 strong. The general advance of the Rebel line is threatening our hold on Missouri and Kentucky. Cincinnati is in danger. Disgust with our present government (and military leadership) is certainly universal.

The Southerners claimed that they knew why their fortunes were soaring in spite of their lack of materiel. They bragged that one Southern boy was worth ten Yankees. They pointed out that the majority of Southern soldiers had grown up on farms where they had picked up the skills necessary for soldiering: shooting, riding, camping, hiking, stalking, and killing. They raised chickens, pigs, cattle, and hogs and then slaughtered them with their

A young private in the Confederate army solemnly poses for a photograph. The rural lifestyle of the South, where young men grew up accustomed to shooting, riding, and killing on the farm, often made them more prepared to enter the army than their Northern counterparts.

own hands for the meat. In short, Southern boys had grown up accustomed to blood, death, and survival, and they could live on very little when they had to.

Although many Northern soldiers had grown up on farms, too, a great number had not. These young men worked as clerks and merchants, fishermen and sailors, craftsmen and factory hands. Although these backgrounds could breed men of courage and determination, as a rule Northerners were less familiar with guns, horses, and camping out than their Southern counterparts.

Reasons to Fight

But perhaps more important than the way in which the Rebels had been raised was the attitude with which they regarded the Yankees. Quite simply, they viewed them as trespassers and invaders, as foreign aggressors coming down from a strange and distant land to threaten their homes and families. The Confederates were fighting for their land and their way of life. The Yankee cause, the preservation of the Union, seemed an abstraction that bore no flesh or bone. However, thus far all the battles had been waged in the South, and the Southerners' wives and children had been and still were endangered; the Confederate soldiers were defending their families as ferociously as did the beasts of the wild.

As one Southerner pointed out:

Our men must prevail or lose their property, country, freedom, everything. On the other hand, the enemy, in yielding the contest, may retire to their own country, and possess everything they enjoyed before the war began.

But perhaps a captured Confederate gave the best response when Federals asked him his reason for fighting. He simply drawled, "I'm fightin' 'cause your down here."

Although slavery may have propelled the politicians into war, it had little to do with why the average Southerner or Northerner enlisted in the beginning. Most Rebel soldiers did not even own slaves, and Abraham Lincoln himself had not made slavery much of an issue. Addressing Congress on July 4, 1861, he had stated that he had "no purpose, directly or indirectly, to interfere with slavery in the States where it exists." Indeed, saving the Union was uppermost among his justifications for conducting the war. In 1862 Lincoln said:

If I could save the Union without freeing any slave, I would do it; if I could save it by freeing all the slaves, I would do it; and if I could save it by freeing some and leaving others alone, I would also do that.

Clearly, the average Northerners were not fighting over the slaves, even though the power struggles between slave and free states had been the principal cause of the war. The common Union soldiers were fighting to prevent the breakup of their one mighty nation into two smaller, less important countries.

Of course, the Confederates had a different viewpoint. They were resisting what they believed was an overly powerful central government's attempt to coerce eleven free and sovereign states into a bond against their will. As Southerners viewed the situation, the Yankee invasion of their homes was part of a power-mad scheme to rule over the entire continent; the Rebel soldiers believed that they had not only a right but also a moral obligation to defend their "states' rights."

At the beginning of the war, President Abraham Lincoln focused on preserving the faltering Union, not abolishing slavery.

THE "SECESSION MOVEMENT".

A cartoon from the Civil War era derides states for breaking away from the Union. Yankees equated secession with treason and supported the army's efforts to keep the Union intact.

The states' rights argument had been coursing through debates, editorials, and the halls of Congress for years and served as a foundation for clashes not only over slavery but also over many other contentious issues. The proponents of states' rights (mostly in the South) believed that each state was like a little country with all the rights, privileges, and responsibilities associated with a sovereign and independent government. They claimed that any particular state could determine its own policies on slavery, taxation, trade, defense, or anything else and that it could leave the Union just as freely as if it were breaking an alliance with a foreign nation.

On the other hand, the North considered the breaking away, or the secession, of the eleven Confederate states at the beginning of the war to be a treasonable act, one that had to be subdued by military force. Northerners believed that the Federal government in Washington, D.C., made up of the president, the Congress of the United States, and the Supreme Court, had ultimate authority over all the states. Most Northerners also believed that such authority was necessary to maintain the United States as a Union strong enough to fulfill its manifest destiny. This was the belief that the United States was destined to take control of

"In God's Good Time"

During the Lincoln-Douglas debates of 1858, Abraham Lincoln repeated in speech after speech that he did not favor the immediate abolition of slavery. Instead, he articulated the majority position in the North by saying, "I am not, nor ever have been, in favor of bringing about in any way the social and political equality of the white and black races. Emancipation will come in God's good time."

His hope, and that of many other Northern politicians, was to avoid war by allowing slavery to continue in the Southern states. He wanted to prevent its spread into the western territories and let the institution die a natural death "in God's good time," which he assumed would be soon.

Lincoln based his trust in the gradual death of slavery on an apparent worldwide trend. Great Britain had outlawed slavery in its colonies during the 1830s. Spain had done the same in the early 1800s, and the French colonies freed the last of their slaves in 1848. It seemed likely that the trend would reach the shores of the American South and that reason would prevail over war.

What Lincoln may not have considered was that human bondage was still thriving in Brazil, Cuba, Puerto Rico, and in large areas of Africa, Asia, and South America (where it is still commonly practiced today). Also, the slave trade was continuing to thrive economically in the Southern United States where slave

Rather than actively pursuing the emancipation of Southern slaves, Abraham Lincoln bided his time, believing slavery would cease on its own.

labor produced profits for plantation owners. Plantations were expanding as never before, and the value of a good slave had skyrocketed. No, American slavery wasn't about to die out "in God's good time" unless, of course, God's timetable included the Civil War.

enough territory to stretch from the Atlantic to the Pacific. Most Northerners thought that the United States should become a continental and even a world power. These were the fundamental reasons that, for the first eighteen months of the war, the North had been invading the South.

The Reasons Change

In September 1862 however, it seemed that everything was changing. For the first time in the war, the Rebels were preparing to invade the North (Maryland). How could the Confederates justify that, many of them wondered, with their commitment to defensive warfare only? Indeed, it was the Yankees now who would be defending their homes, for no one expected Robert E. Lee's invasion to stop in Maryland. Pennsylvania would surely be next and, who knew, maybe the rest of the North as well.

Nearly all the Southerners were uncomfortable with the idea of leaving the South to fight on what they called foreign territory. A chaplain reported that "many believed as a matter of prudence at least that we should not leave our own soil: that it looked a little like invasion. A large number hung back and would not cross the (Potomac) river."

The impending Southern invasion was not the only reason the tables were turning. As far back as early July 1862, President Lincoln had prepared a document that would radically change the character of the war, should he ever get the chance to announce it. Lincoln's words would raise the Federal cause from a political to a moral one and transform his men from invaders to holy crusaders.

Lincoln had planned to issue this policy change in midsummer, but all his armies were in retreat at that time. His advisors told him that his proclamation would look like a last pathetic shriek of defeat if he announced it while the Confederates were chasing his troops out of Virginia. The president needed a victory, and he needed it soon. It had to come in Maryland. Only then from a position of strength and reversed momentum could he introduce his decree to the world.

Lincoln called his decree the Emancipation Proclamation, and with it he would at last officially dedicate himself and the United States to freeing the slaves (or at least some of them). As an initial step, he would be emancipating the slaves held in states and parts of states still in open rebellion against the Union.

The proclamation, he calculated, would also benefit his stumbling war effort. It would encourage field hands to run away from the plantations, thereby reducing the South's agricultural output, perhaps to the point of starving out the Rebel armies. Further, European nations that had been considering giving foreign aid to the Confederacy would not dare do so once the Rebel cause was redefined as one to maintain slavery.

Consequently, a great deal was at stake before the battle in Maryland. For the Confederates, victory meant help from Europe, relief for war-ravaged Virginia, and a chance at a negotiated peace settlement. For the Union, a win might mean even more: the beginning of the end of slavery, noninterference from Europe, and renewed hopes for preserving the Union.

September 17, 1862, was destined to become the bloodiest day in American history, the first true turning point of the Civil War. Which side would ultimately prevail, and which side's losses would be the bloodiest? No one could answer these questions in the warm, lazy days of the Civil War's second summer, least of all the soldiers in blue and gray who were converging on Sharpsburg, Maryland, a little town along a little creek that Native Americans had named Antietam.

CHAPTER TWO

Delay at South Mountain

The roads that would eventually lead to Sharpsburg and Antietam Creek passed through the well-manicured city of Frederick, Maryland. General Lee and his army reached its steepled skyline well ahead of the sluggish McClellan. Once there, Lee camped his army for three days, allowing them to rest, heal their blistered feet, and try to get the lice out of their clothing. He was careful not to let his men loose in the town's cobbled streets, though, for fear that their foraging for local food would alienate the citizens.

The allegiances of Maryland were still untried; however, slavery had long existed in the state, and it was reasonable for Lee to assume that the residents might be willing and even eager to side with the Confederacy. Indeed, Southern sympathizers in Baltimore had rioted and killed Union soldiers at the beginning of the war as the Yankee recruits attempted to make their way to Washington. And the Federals still considered it necessary to garrison troops throughout the state as much to prevent an uprising by Marylanders as to prevent an invasion by Confederates.

Those garrison troops may have discouraged any attempts by Southern-sympathizing Marylanders to rise up in revolution, but they had done little to slow down General Lee's advance toward Frederick. Although there had been a few minor skirmishes between the Rebels and the more numerous Yankee troops, the fights did little more to impede the Confederate advance than a few boys throwing rocks might have. General Lee, nonetheless, viewed his winning the skirmishes as the first noble steps toward liberating a potential ally.

For his part, Abraham Lincoln feared losing Maryland enough to suspend the writ of habeas corpus and imprison thirteen thousand Southern-leaning judges, politicians, editors, and law-enforcement personnel without giving them a trial from 1861 to 1863. Even most Northerners considered that to be an unconstitutional act, and Lincoln's popularity suffered greatly because of it. The fact that he went ahead and imprisoned these "secessionist agitators" suggests just how real he considered the threat of Maryland's "going South" to be. After all, if Maryland seceded, the Federal capital at Washington would be completely surrounded by enemy territory. At that time, capturing the enemy's capital was nearly the same as winning the war.

The ultimate, strategic advantages to the South's winning over Maryland were not lost on anyone, least of all Robert E. Lee. Neither were the more immediate benefits such as the acquisition of food, horses, supplies, and men. As part of his efforts to woo the border state's wavering allegiances, General Lee issued the following proclamation to the people of Maryland:

In a proclamation to the people of Maryland, Confederate general Robert E. Lee eloquently solicited the state's secession and invited its citizens to revolt from the "foreign yoke" of the Union government.

> The people of the Confederate States have long watched the wrongs and outrages which have been inflicted upon the citizens of a commonwealth allied to the states of the South by the strongest social, political, and commercial ties and, believing that the people of Maryland possess a spirit too lofty to submit to such a government, the people of the South wish to aid you in throwing off this foreign yoke. There will be no constraint or intimidation; this army will respect your choice, whatever it may be; and while the Southern people will rejoice to welcome you to your natural position among them, they will only welcome you when you come of your own free will.

McClellan's Most Lasting Contribution

General George McClellan undoubtedly left his mark on the Union Army of the Potomac. No one will ever be able to deny that it was his organizational talent and his strength of will that molded that dispirited mob into a magnificent fighting force. On the other hand, he will also be remembered for his mishandling of that army in battle.

Perhaps, however, neither of these facts lingered longer in the minds of the common soldiers in the cavalry than the fact that McClellan was an inventor. For one of the versatile general's most lasting accomplishments rested in the improvements he made to the saddle.

McClellan had spent time as a cavalryman before the war and had grown weary of the existing model. It was heavy, cumbersome to strap on, and caused discomfort to some of a soldier's most tender and sensitive spots.

While observing the European cavalry during the Crimean War, he noticed that their saddles were lighter, more comfortable, and much simpler in design than the American version. The European cavalrymen, to his surprise, rarely complained of saddle soreness.

He soon went to work and reinvented the U.S. Army saddle with a design that became so popular that Confederate cavalry men conducted raids specifically to steal Northern saddles. The U.S. Cavalry, though, paid the general the ultimate tribute. For the remaining seventy years of its existence, the cavalry never replaced or improved upon the McClellan saddle, and it is still in use among civilian riders today.

In addition to being a talented leader, General George McClellan was also a gifted inventor. His revolutionary saddle design was made popular by the U.S. Cavalry and remains in use today.

The response was lukewarm. Southern supporters turned out in appreciable numbers bearing a variety of much-needed supplies. Gowned women and petticoated girls brought flowers, cakes, meats, and pies while men shared liquor and cigars. But in spite of this welcome, General Lee could tell that most of the people in the western part of Maryland remained loyal to the Union. He quickly wrote to Confederate President Jefferson Davis, "I do not anticipate any general rising of the people in our behalf." At least one other Confederate general was finding out the same thing—and in a much more dangerous manner.

Lee Makes a Bold Move

General J. E. B. Stuart's Rebel cavalry had been skirmishing with small groups of Federal cavalry for several days, but now the plume-hatted cavalier reported back that the main body of McClellan's army was finally approaching Frederick. It was time to act, General Lee decided, and he set about devising his riskiest scheme yet.

Counting on McClellan's customarily slow pace, Lee drew up Special Orders No. 191, a plan to divide his already smaller army into four separate commands each with its own distinct mission. He would send General James Longstreet, his strong and silent "war horse," on ahead toward Pennsylvania to start the invasion there. The eccentric professor "Stonewall" Jackson, who earned his nickname by resisting the enemy like a stone wall, would turn south and capture the twelve-thousand-man garrison threatening the Rebels' supply and communication lines at Harpers Ferry, Virginia. Lee ordered the grumbling D. H. Hill to cover the Confederate army's rear after it crossed a couple of gaps on top of South Mountain; Lee would follow Longstreet into Pennsylvania.

To anyone with even a semblance of military training (which, of course, included all of Lee's generals) the plan appeared foolhardy. It was common knowledge that a commander should never divide his force in the face of an enemy, especially when the enemy had twice as many guns. But no one objected as Lee laid out his plan in the orange lamplight of his tent: not the bearish Longstreet, not Jackson with his many quirks, not even the constantly grousing D. H. Hill.

Confederate general J. E. B. Stuart (pictured) alerted General Lee that Union troops were approaching Frederick; this news prompted Lee to divide his forces as part of a risky scheme to defeat the Yankees.

The reason was simple: trust. Thus far, General Lee's strategies had pushed the Yankees out of Virginia and forced them on the defensive in their own homeland. No one was going to question his wisdom now. General Lee's subordinates received their orders without protest, and the columns began to march on September 10.

"At four o'clock in the morning," a Union sympathizer wrote, "the Rebel army began to move from our town, Jackson's force taking the advance. We were anxious to get rid of [Jackson's force] and the penetrating ammoniacal smell they brought with them." Noticing all the equipment they had captured from previous fighting, he added bitterly, "This Rebel army seems to have been largely supplied by the United States Quartermaster!"

The Saviors Arrive

General McClellan's lumbering army began to shuffle into Frederick on September 12. It entered to a hero's reception of banners, flags, and jubilant cheers. If there had been any doubt as to the loyalty of western Maryland, it was put to rest this day. The people of Frederick obviously loved the Union, and they regarded the general as their deliverer.

"Handkerchiefs are raised," a townsman wrote. "Flags are flown from Union houses, and a new life appears infused into the people." A young Union soldier said, "The place was alive with girls going around the streets in squads waving flags, singing songs, and inviting the soldiers in for hot suppers."

McClellan lapped up the glory, being careful to maintain his aloof and superior demeanor. He enjoyed the attention so much, in fact, that he lingered in Frederick longer than he should have. President Lincoln had to send him another in a series of telegraph messages urging him to pursue the Rebels before they slipped any farther north.

But it seemed the general had God's blessing if not the president's when a couple of his men stumbled upon the find that would certainly assure a Yankee victory. While camping in an area previously occupied by the Southerners, these men spotted what appeared to be several cigars wrapped in a paper. They both scrambled for the prize and wrestled briefly over it until one of them realized that there were plans of some kind on the wrapping paper. They were the plans of the Rebels!

Somehow a copy of Lee's Special Orders No. 191 had been left behind, and McClellan soon held in his hands the entire Confederate plan for splitting up its army. "Now I know what to do!" he cried out from his tent. "Here is the paper with which if I cannot whip Bobbie Lee, I will be willing to go home!"

But despite his bluster, General McClellan wasted another day in camp before heading west toward South Mountain. He

A Poor Showing for Stonewall

General Thomas J. "Stonewall" Jackson was already a military legend by the time he reached Frederick, Maryland. However, if part of General Lee's reason for coming to Frederick was to win friends for the Confederacy, then Stonewall failed dismally to do his part on at least one occasion.

It was on a Sunday night when he decided to attend church in town. Still aching from a fall from his horse, he took an ambulance wagon to the service. The detail of cavalry and aides who escorted him to the door made a particularly noisy caravan, and the commotion outside disrupted the service that was already in progress.

Stiff and sore, Jackson added to the ruckus by limping heavily all the way down to the front pew. When he finally looked up, he saw that the minister was angrily waiting for him to get settled and eyeing him with a Unionist's contempt. Jackson said nothing as the preacher pointedly offered up a long-winded prayer for Abraham Lincoln and the Federal armies. In fact, the general barely noticed. He had already nodded off, snoring as he always did in church and drooling down his dull beard.

Inspired by reports from an offended congregation, a flurry of newspaper articles cast aspersions not only on Jackson but also on the cause he so boorishly represented. If any Marylanders had been considering switching their support to the South, this publicity did little to encourage them. It would remain to be seen, however, whether a lack of social graces would impair this slovenly man's ability to command soldiers in battle.

General "Stonewall" Jackson's lack of social graces offended Marylanders in Frederick when he disrupted a church service and nodded off during the sermon.

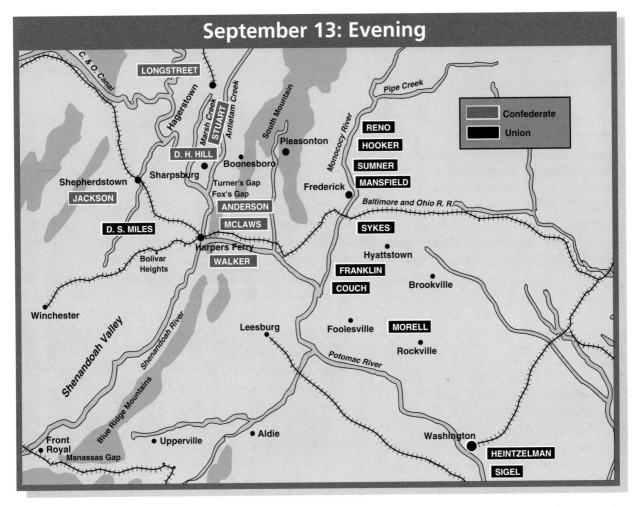

September 13: Evening

Confederate	
Union	

(Map labels: C. & O. Canal, LONGSTREET, Hagerstown, Marsh Creek, Antietam Creek, STUART, South Mountain, Pipe Creek, Monocacy River, RENO, Pleasonton, HOOKER, Boonesboro, D. H. HILL, SUMNER, Sharpsburg, Turner's Gap, MANSFIELD, Shepherdstown, Fox's Gap, Frederick, Baltimore and Ohio R. R., JACKSON, ANDERSON, MCLAWS, D. S. MILES, SYKES, Harpers Ferry, Hyattstown, Bolivar Heights, WALKER, FRANKLIN, COUCH, Brookville, Winchester, Shenandoah Valley, Shenandoah River, Leesville, Foolesville, MORELL, Potomac River, Rockville, Blue Ridge Mountains, Front Royal, Upperville, Aldie, Manassas Gap, Washington, HEINTZELMAN, SIGEL)

boasted that he would cross the mountain (actually a long, high ridge) and beat Lee's dispersed forces. Even with the needless forfeiture of a day, McClellan had every chance of doing just that. First, however, his eighty thousand men would have to sweep aside D. H. Hill and the three thousand Confederates guarding the passes. But how much trouble could that be?

Lee Reacts

That night, one of J. E. B. Stuart's spies reported that McClellan had found the lost order and was planning to advance the next day. Throwing himself up on his horse, the flamboyant Stuart rode hard, his red-lined cape flapping in the night air, to report the news personally to General Lee.

Lee immediately knew what he must do. It would take time, time he did not have, but he needed to reassemble his total force of forty thousand men. If he could just wrest two days from the Yankees, perhaps he could at least get Longstreet back down to some central location where all the other parts of the divided army could reunite with him.

Greener Pastures?

The plight of the slaves in the South is as well documented as their dreams of running away to a better life in the North. But did they really find that better life in the Northern cities? Did escaping from slavery truly set them free?

As the U.S. Army freed slaves and sent them North, many newspapers there tried to stir up passions against them. One paper brashly displayed its ugly prejudice by saying that the Yankees should be "willing to fight for Uncle Sam but not for Uncle Sambo."

Though freed from their Southern masters, Blacks arriving in the North soon discovered that many things had not changed at all. One former slave in Wisconsin was lynched by a mob shouting, "Damn the niggers and abolitionists!" His crime—winning a fist fight.

Blacks found themselves excluded by custom, if not by law, from nearly every facet of White society. Black abolitionist Frederick Douglass pointed out indignantly that Philadelphia, the City of Brotherly Love, had "its white schools and colored schools, its white churches and its colored churches, its white Christianity and its colored Christianity."

The disease-infested ghettos in which Blacks were forced to live reeked with stench and rot. Tar paper huts crawling with rats offered the only shelter, summer or winter, and these sad-eyed ragamuffins got little help from Northerners or Southerners.

Perhaps, though, the Northern factory workers, many of whom were recent immigrants themselves, hated the Black people most bitterly. They believed that the former slaves, accustomed to working hard for very little, would replace them in their jobs, which in many cases is exactly what happened. Irish factory workers eventually rioted against the Blacks in New York City, killing 150 and burning out hundreds more before being put down by U.S. soldiers.

The former slaves, around whom many of the causes of the war revolved, were not accepted in either the North or the South. Sadly, it would take another hundred years before the Black race would even begin to be treated justly in America.

Many former slaves fled the South, hoping to find better treatment in the North; however, Black factory workers (pictured) in the North continued to be plagued by prejudice and oppression.

On the map, the little town of Sharpsburg appeared to be in the central location Lee needed and it offered a ford, or shallow place, across the Potomac River if Lee's army should need an escape route. Maybe Longstreet could make a stand at Sharpsburg with half the army, Lee thought, just long enough to get Jackson up from Harpers Ferry with the other half. He wanted to give Stonewall those two precious days to complete his capture of the Union garrison at Harpers Ferry before calling him up to Sharpsburg.

As confusing as the situation was, General Lee grasped it fully and acted decisively. He needed two days with which to save his army and perhaps turn a near disaster into some sort of triumph. He must have two days, and it looked like he might just get them. McClellan's delay in Frederick gave him the first day. He would have to rely on the irritable D. H. Hill to purchase him the second.

The Battle of South Mountain

Sunday, September 14, dawned blue skied and bright atop South Mountain, Maryland. The troops could hear church bells tolling in the distance, and birdsong filled the invigorating air. General McClellan had sent two brigades up to South Mountain during the night, and they were ready for battle by 9:00 A.M. The five thousand Yankees expected to meet at least that many Confederates, but here at Fox's Gap, a mile south of the main crossing at Turner's Gap, the Northerners found barely one thousand Southerners crouched behind a stone wall.

After what seemed an eternity to men on both sides, the Federals marched across the open, rocky field, drums beating and flags waving. The Rebels hid behind the wall, their guns primed and loaded, sweating in their jackets. The fight began with coordinated volleys from both forces but dissolved into a ripping, tearing melee of men loading and firing at will. Soldiers tumbled in shrieking agony during charge after thrown-back charge.

Fear and confusion tumbled into a gathering swirl of mayhem filled with shouting officers, riderless horses, and bleeding men clutching at their bodies. Artillerists swabbed barrels, cannonballs sucked air, bullets tore into flesh. Amid the vomiting and curses, the pleas and the moans, and the clouds that reeked of sulfur, the six thousand brave, frightened men and boys packed into their lines trying to load their weapons and fire them.

Those whose barrels did not foul up with powder residue and whose hands were not shaking too badly could fire about three times per minute. Most, however, could only manage to fire twice in that time. Even at that rate, some ten thousand hissing bullets were sometimes being exchanged in a sixty-second period. The Rebels, who were taking the majority of the bullets behind their stone wall, kept up a daunting return fire and showed no signs of yielding.

From Dishonor to Dignity

General Robert E. Lee owned the Arlington House, a magnificent plantation mansion overlooking Washington, D.C. It had been built by George Washington's stepson and had passed down to General Lee through his wife who was descended from the same lineage.

The Union army took over the grand estate at the outset of the war and used it as a headquarters until the U.S. Army quartermaster general decided to dishonor the "traitorous Confederate general." The officer ordered that the lovely grounds be dug up and used as a cemetery, fouling the soil with the decomposing bodies of Federal soldiers who had died, as he believed, at Lee's hands.

General Lee would have had the last laugh, though, if he had lived to see what eventually became of his plantation. For it was transformed into one of the most patriotic and sacred pieces of ground in America: Arlington National Cemetery, the final resting place of our nation's greatest military heroes.

Union soldiers lounge on the steps and lawn of General Lee's spectacular mansion, Arlington House. Lee's expansive plantation was later transformed into the Arlington National Cemetery.

The Federals out in the open were suffering more casualties, the dead dropping from their lines as they advanced and fell back, but the Rebels were suffering too, with horribly maimed faces, heads, and hands. For two hours the battle went back and forth, neither side able to gain an advantage, until an Ohio regiment led by Colonel Rutherford B. Hayes outflanked the Confederates and swooped down on them in a hand-to-hand bloodbath. One Federal soldier wrote, "We rushed into them and all the time every man shouting as loud as he could. I got rather more excited than I ever wish to again."

Men shot their rifles and swung them like clubs. They plunged bayonets into bellies and chests. Screaming and wailing, they knifed, punched, and strangled in this gnashing cauldron of pain and hate. Swordsmen lashed out like crazed, cornered animals. Every man cursed, moaned, and shrieked until finally the Confederates fell back, leaving the equally ravaged Yankees in possession of the wall and the heaps of dead around their feet.

The battle raged on throughout the day all along South Mountain with the Rebels demanding a high price for every foot of ground they yielded. Both sides poured in reinforcements

The introduction of rifles changed warfare dramatically and resulted in an incredibly high number of casualties.

A Colonel Like Any Other

There was nothing particularly special about the regimental commander of the Twenty-third Ohio. True, he had been a spelling champion in grammar school, a literary scholar in college, and a lawyer in his early twenties, but none of those credentials set him apart in any significant way. Preferring literature to the law, he nearly starved to death in his first few years of practice.

At the outset of the war, he joined the army and rose through the ranks like other young men. But his rise was less because of his military prowess than for the fact that all the officers ahead of him had been killed. Again, nothing special. It happened all the time.

A year of guerrilla actions in West Virginia had hardened this bookworm a bit, and by the time the Battle of South Mountain rolled around, he was chafing for a full-on fight (still, like all the rest). He finally got his fight, a flanking charge that drove the Rebels back, but he paid for it dearly. While shouting "Give 'em hell, boys! Give the sons of bitches hell!" an explosion of pain ripped through his left arm with the force of a locomotive.

A Rebel minié ball had lacerated his flesh and shattered the upper bones. He went down hard, lapsing into black, bottomless agony like the hundreds of others writhing on this field.

The army sent him back to Ohio, and while he was convalescing at home the newspapers made something of a hero of him (along with the help of some enterprising politicians). The voters soon elected him to be their congressman and then their governor, and eventually the nineteenth president of the United States. His name? Rutherford B. Hayes—maybe he was just a little bit special.

Years after his heroic efforts at the Battle of South Mountain, Rutherford B. Hayes was elected president of the United States.

(eight thousand for the Confederates and eighteen thousand for the Federals), but still General McClellan did not make a concentrated advance. If he had, instead of cautiously probing with one brigade at a time, the Federals would certainly have broken through Confederate lines.

However, the Federals did not push, and nightfall ended the carnage. The Rebels had held on by an eyelash. Having paid in blood for that extra day General Lee needed, D. H. Hill ordered his surviving men to fall back during the night and join Lee at Sharpsburg.

The Yankees, who had fought every bit as ferociously as the Confederates, lay down among the lifeless and wounded to sleep. But the moans and cries kept the Northern troops awake all night long as did the sniping of Rebel sharpshooters.

By sunrise on September 15, the Federals held South Mountain and were beginning their descent into the valley of Antietam. Sharpsburg, where the enemy was known to be gathering, lay just six miles ahead. Morale was high. The casualties—eighteen hundred Union and twenty-three hundred Confederate—and the Rebel withdrawal suggested that the North had won the battle. Each time General McClellan appeared to his men, they sang and cheered him grandly. "It was like a great scene in a play," wrote an officer, "with the roar of the guns for accompaniment." Soon, that officer was sure, the Federals would crush the insolent rebellion forever.

As General Lee watched the Union vanguard arrive across Antietam Creek, he was thinking much the same thing. He had only half his army present, and Jackson was running a day late at Harpers Ferry. For all of D. H. Hill's efforts, Lee still needed another twenty-four hours. Should he stay here and fight the Yankees without the extra time, he wondered; the Yankees outnumbered the Rebels four to one. Should he instead retreat back into Virginia and return another time? Lee's decision would depend upon his assessment of two very different commanders, Stonewall Jackson and George McClellan, and on which of them could get his men to Sharpsburg first.

CHAPTER THREE

The Bloodiest Day Dawns

Colonel Dixon S. Miles, commander of the Union garrison at Harpers Ferry, had spent two long, sleepless nights surrounded by Stonewall Jackson's troops, and the effects of the siege showed. A longtime alcoholic now struggling to dry out, the white-bearded old man possessed none of the fire that had made him such a fine professional soldier during the Mexican War and the Indian campaigns.

He had poorly deployed his twelve thousand men, placing very few on the heights looming over the little community. As a result, seventy-five big Confederate guns encircled him, and they were booming away at will. It would only be a matter of time,

Stonewall Jackson and his Rebel troops stormed the small West Virginia town of Harpers Ferry (pictured), forcing the Union troops to surrender in defeat.

he knew, before the Rebel infantry came swarming down on him, and he had no faith in the ability of his inexperienced troops to stop the Confederates.

His only hope was to be rescued by a Federal breakthrough on South Mountain. That breakthrough, however, had been delayed by one crucial day, all but assuring his own defeat. As he wrestled with his nerves, surrender seemed his only option. Some of his cavalry had refused that option and boldly escaped during the night, but he knew his infantry would have no chance of escaping.

All that remained for him to do was raise the white flags of shame. Thousands of handkerchiefs soon joined in all along the Union front indicating that the Yankee soldiers seemed more relieved than ashamed. Miles had lost Harpers Ferry and the freedom of his men, and soon he would lose his own life. Before the Rebel guns could all be silenced, a shell exploded behind him. The blast nearly severed one of his legs, and he died in agony the next day.

Stonewall Jackson lost little time in making his way into Harpers Ferry, though he did so with very little fanfare. A Northern reporter commented:

> He was dressed in the coarsest kind of homespun, seedy and dirty at that; wore an old hat which any northern beggar would consider an insult to have offered him, and in general appearance was in no respect to be distinguished from the mongrel, bare-footed crew who follows his fortunes!

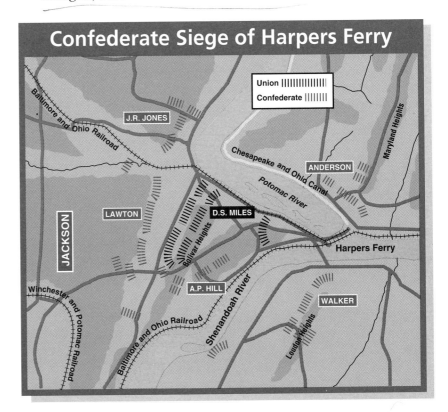

Confederate Siege of Harpers Ferry

The dauntless generals of the Confederate army, Robert E. Lee (left) and Stonewall Jackson. Under Jackson's able command, the Rebels crushed the Yankees at Harpers Ferry.

Most Federals thought the same thing of "the mighty Stonewall." One soldier observed, "Boys, he is not much for looks but if he had been in command of us we would not have been caught in this trap."

Ignoring the cheers of his own men, Jackson quickly set about arranging the surrender. He ordered General A. P. Hill and his division to remain behind to confiscate the Yankees' supplies and weapons and then catch up with him as soon as possible. Stonewall had gotten several dispatches from General Lee imploring him to hurry to Sharpsburg, and he did not want to waste another minute.

General Jackson issued marching orders and started north to cover the eighteen miles back into Maryland. One of his foot cavalry remarked, "He gave us a musket, 100 rounds, and a gum blanket [rubberized ground cloth] and he drove us like hell!" Even pushing his men that way, he knew he might not be able to reunite with Lee before the great clash began. Jackson assumed that A. P. Hill's division would miss the fight altogether.

"Have You Seen the Elephant?"

The brutal campaigns of the first eighteen months of the war cost both armies thousands and thousands of men. Many others volunteered to take their places, but few of the replacements had combat experience. As the green recruits arrived in camp, the veterans chided them, "Have you seen the elephant yet, boys? Well, don't you worry none. The circus is just up ahead. And that there elephant's a'waitin' for you!"

The new boys were not exactly sure what the veterans were talking about, but they quickly and frightfully got the picture. "Seeing the elephant" was a reference to the shock they had all presumably felt as children when they witnessed the huge, tusked beasts for the first time.

One seasoned tough would later say, "Before the Antietam campaign, I'd only seen tame elephants and small ones at that." Within the next few days, recruits and veterans alike would not only see but also be trampled by an elephant far more horrible and terrifying than any other of the war.

A soldier establishes a vantage point as the Confederate and Union forces face off on the rolling hills of Sharpsburg, thus beginning the bloody Battle of Antietam.

End of the Wait

General McClellan won the race to Antietam Creek but, as usual, did not capitalize on his advantage. While Jackson was still on the march, Little Mac had seventy thousand men ready to attack Lee's twenty thousand, but he chose instead to wait another day.

That was all the time that Generals Lee and Jackson needed. On the evening of September 16, Lee welcomed his favorite commander, his "right arm," warmly to Sharpsburg, where he placed him on the Confederate left flank in a clump of forest called the West Woods. The North still outnumbered the South two to one as the Army of Northern Virginia settled in for an anxious sleep less than a mile from the massive Union force.

Those who could not sleep (and there were many) huddled around fires, speaking softly if they spoke at all. Some wrote letters or reread old ones. Even the atheists prayed. Pages rattled, from the Bible mostly. Occasionally, a man stumbled off to vomit. Very few men played cards or drank or swore. Even the most hardened veterans did not want to tempt the Lord.

When dawn finally broke on September 17, it was a misty and steely gray day. The five hundred Union and Confederate artillery pieces began to pound. One colonel remarked that the fire "grew so rapid . . . from both sides that it became one prolonged roar." Another man said simply, "It was artillery hell."

With fiery explosions throwing body parts about, Jackson ordered the first of his divisions out into line. These three thousand men formed a half-mile-long double line along the edge of a rolling farm field owned by a man named Miller. The rocky pasture just before them was cleared, but a huge cornfield filled the expanse beyond. Stonewall sent a regiment down into that head-high corn to serve as a forward line.

Men tensed and sweat as the big guns resounded. Nervous skirmishing broke out along the East Woods to the right. Throats dried, trousers wet, brave men trembled and shook, as well they should have, with cannon blasts evaporating a half-dozen men at a time. Flashing their frightened eyes toward every incoming round, the men flinched, waiting for the worst. The Southerners did not have to wait long, for out of the North Woods a mile straight ahead came the drums, fifes, bugles, and officer calls of ten thousand bayonet-wielding Yankees.

The Federals Push First

Major General Joseph Hooker aimed his Union First Corps across the broad cornfield at what looked like a little, white-brick schoolhouse. It was actually Dunker Church, but out of modest piety, the total-immersion Baptist congregation had not built a steeple, so most soldiers referred to it throughout the battle as "the schoolhouse." Hooker himself was swearing loudly at his men, berating any who fell behind. Between long drinks of whiskey and draws on his cigar, he cursed anything and everything that might even remotely need cursing while struggling to keep himself upright in the saddle.

(Below) Soldiers form the Confederate forward line to begin their march through Miller's cornfield. Meanwhile, General Joseph Hooker (pictured) positions his Union forces to meet the Southern onslaught with deadly cannon fire.

Then the Confederates positioned on a hill to the right of the Union forces opened up. A New Yorker wrote, "The fire and smoke, flashing of muskets and whizzing of bullets, yells of men were all perfectly horrible." A Massachusetts man added, "The shot and shell fell among us thick and fast. I don't see how any of us got out alive."

Nevertheless, General Hooker, leading by fiery example, pushed his men onward until a glint of bayonets in the corn ahead riveted his hawkish stare. He saw the Rebels that Jackson had sent forward into the corn standing at attention like so many bowling pins. Whether they were unaware that the Yankees were closing or were too foolish to care, General Hooker did not know. But he wasted no time in bringing up thirty-six of his deadliest cannon with which to dispatch them into the next world.

Loading the big guns with cannister, or musket balls that turned each piece into a giant shotgun, Hooker raked the field with one shuddering blast, instantly reducing five hundred bright-eyed Southerners to a heap of bloody rags. Hooker later wrote:

> Every stalk of corn was cut as closely as could have been done with a knife and the slain lay in rows precisely where they had stood in their ranks a few moments before. It was never my fortune to witness a more bloody, dismal battlefield.

Thus, the first phase of the Battle of Antietam began.

Thousands of Confederates to the front opened up on the Federals. The Federals aligned themselves and returned volley after volley until eighteen thousand rifles, North and South, were hard at work. "Never did I see more Rebs to fire at than at that moment presented themselves," said one Yankee. "It was a hot time for us and most of our Regiment was used up in a very short time."

The noise alone made heads throb. It seemed the sky was tumbling down. A war correspondent noted that the crashing "merged into a tumultuous chorus that made the earth tremble. The discharge of musketry sounded upon the ear like the rolling of a thousand drums." Clouds of smoke set men to coughing and rendered their stinging eyes nearly useless. But the Yankees charged, shouting their low hurrah, and nearly breached the Rebel line.

Bloody See-Saw

When the Confederates began to crack, Jackson sent in another brigade that chased and blasted the Unionists back to the North Woods. "The men, I cannot say fell," recalled a Union major. "They were knocked out of the ranks by dozens."

More Federals in the North Woods, lying in wait, rose up when the pursuing Rebels burst out of the smoke upon them. The Yankees blew these Southerners away in a succession of

flaming volleys and routed the survivors back toward the church from which they had come. In turn, another brigade of Jackson's screaming men repulsed that charge and mounted a counterattack of their own until they, too, were "cut down as if by a scythe running through [their] lines."

Smoke fills the battlefield and shrouds Dunker Church as the Union troops charge toward the Confederates.

The battle went back and forth for three endless, aching hours. The Unionists charged and nearly shattered the Southern line only to be driven back by Jackson's well-timed replacements. But those Confederate replacements never reformed their own lines. They would pursue the running Yankees, wailing their high-pitched rebel yell, only to be mowed down by the next set of Federal reserves who, in turn, would start the whole bloody cycle over again.

The see-sawing horrors shocked even the most battle-seasoned survivors. They tried to look away whenever they could, but after a while there was no place to look away to. Carnage was everywhere. A Union officer watched an exploding shell "send a naked arm 30 feet into the air only to fall back down and land beside me. It was awful . . . just awful." One Confederate officer noticed a slowly walking mount apparently dragging its rider by the stirrup. "But to my horror," he discovered,

J. E. B. Stuart's Ball

Major General James Ewell Brown Stuart represented all that a Southern cavalryman was meant to be. He was young, handsomely bearded, jovial in every situation, and the very symbol of plantation gentility. He led boisterous sing-alongs and played pranks on his men when he was not bowing to every passing lady. He loved to dance and sought out parties or threw them himself.

Such was the case during his stay near Frederick when he decided to hold a Southern-style ball. Accordingly, Stuart took over an abandoned girls' academy and decorated it with crossed sabers and flags. When the brass band arrived, he sent his officers to fetch the local ladies, properly chaperoned, of course. The quadrilles, waltzes, and reels then began amid a flutter of titters and sighs.

The mood was shattered, though, when a panting sergeant rushed in and announced that Yankee cavalrymen were firing on the pickets, or soldiers on guard duty. After a short but formal exchange of good-byes, the officers snatched their sabers from the walls and bounded away.

This very minor military incident ended the ball much earlier than planned, but as one belle said, "One hour's acquaintance in war time goes further towards good feeling than months in the dull, slow periods of peace." In less than a week, many of the belles would be saddened at the news that their new beaux had danced their final dances before dying on the bloody fields along Antietam Creek.

"the horse was dragging its own entrails from the gaping wound of a cannonball."

By 9:00 A.M. on Wednesday, September 17, Miller's cornfield had changed hands thirteen times, and still neither side could claim an advantage. But each new attack did change at least one thing: The number of broken bodies mounted. General Jackson had started the fight with eight thousand men, and now nearly half of them were down. He had no reserves left. He had committed every single regiment available to him. If the Yankees attacked just one more time, Jackson knew his men could not possibly resist.

General Hooker, himself wounded now, had begun the battle with ten thousand men and had lost four thousand so far. But unlike Lee and Jackson, he had thousands more men in reserve if General McClellan would just let him use some of them. But the ever-cautious McClellan had made his orders clear. He alone would control those extra thirty thousand men. "They are all that stands between Lee and the Capital," he would say throughout the day, and he would not risk even one man against the legendary Stonewall Jackson. He thereby missed the first of many opportunities to crush the Southern army.

Jackson pulled the tattered remains of his command back through to the other side of the West Woods, intending to make a last, defiant stand there when the Yankees returned. He waited and waited; when the charge did not come, he rode up to Miller's cornfield to take a closer look.

The sight he saw would have shocked most men to tears, if nothing else. Before him lay some seven thousand men and boys or the bloody parts that had once been men and boys. Many were crying for their mothers and begging to be put out of their

Facing defeat, General Stonewall Jackson (center) gives orders to his troops during the Battle of Antietam.

misery. They whimpered to God and cursed him in the same breath. But Jackson paid them no attention. Seeing through his field glasses that the Federals had called off their attacks, he said simply, "God has been very kind to us this day."

Slaughter in the West Woods

Intending to switch the focus of his attack away from Jackson and toward the center of the Rebel line, McClellan ordered General Edwin Sumner to advance his division and two others in that direction. However, in the confusion that accompanies all battles, Sumner somehow headed his five thousand men toward Jackson's remnants in the West Woods instead. Crossing Miller's cornfield as if on dress parade, the Union general let his unopposed lines edge dangerously close to one another, dooming any maneuvering they might have to make to certain confusion.

Those were not the only mistakes the cantankerous Sumner was making. He was supposed to wait and attack with the two other divisions, but living up to the nickname he had earned in the Mexican War when a musket ball glanced off his skull, old "Bull Head" became impatient and stormed off alone toward the West Woods with his division.

Even that reduced force, though, should have been enough to mop up Jackson's leftovers. There was no sign of living Confederates anywhere. Crossing the cornfield from the East Woods to the West Woods, one Yankee commented that "you could have walked across the entire field without stepping on nothing but dead men."

The morale of Sumner's soldiers was high. The end was in sight. With any luck at all, the battle would be over in less than thirty minutes. The Yankee boys were singing and joking as they entered the West Woods and descended the tree-darkened hillside.

Some called it bad luck for the Yankees. Others said it was fate. According to Major General Thomas J. Jackson, only God could have ordained such a miracle. When three thousand of the Federals got bogged down among the trees, Southern reinforcements unexpectedly arrived. Having just rushed up from Harpers Ferry, Generals McLaws and Walker's divisions surrounded the West Woods on three sides. They immediately brought their three thousands rifles to bear on the hapless Yankees and poured a murderous fusillade on them.

Within the shadowy woods, a maelstrom erupted. One Yankee reported, "The roar of the rifles was beyond anything conceivable to the uninitiated. If all the stone and brick houses of Broadway should tumble down at once the roar and rattle could hardly be greater." Bullets swarmed like bees. They clipped branches and nicked bark, plowed up furrows in the mulched ground, and ripped through the leaves overhead. But far worse than that, they struck bodies with sickening thuds, seared flesh, and broke bones.

Boys Will Be Boys

During the worst of the fighting in Miller's cornfield, a fourteen-year-old Yankee bugle boy made history. While attached to an artillery battery, Johnnie Cook saved his wounded commander's life by carrying the full-grown man to safety. Cook's valor did not end there.

Under a fire that was dropping Federals all around him, young Cook ran back to the guns where he discovered one was unmanned. Its five-man crew was lying dead, and Confederate infantry were closing fast. Doing the work of all five artillerists, Johnnie sponged, loaded, rammed, primed, aimed, and fired the bellowing field piece. The cannister blasts tore holes in the rebel-yelling lines and slowed their advance but did not stop it.

Cook's valor and determination so inspired a Union general that he jumped down from his horse and pitched in to help. Together, the bugle boy and the general loaded, fired, reloaded, and fired again until the surviving Southerners turned and fled. Cheers went up for the youthful artillerist. The general made note of his name. The officer later wrote that Johnnie's "courage and conduct in that battle won the admiration of all who witnessed it." It also won him the Congressional Medal of Honor.

From the West Woods to the Supreme Court

Captain Oliver Wendell Holmes Jr. of the Twentieth Massachusetts found himself trapped in the same deadly crossfire as all the rest of the Federals being massacred in this wooded hell called the West Woods. As a company commander, he was trying to maintain some semblance of order even though other regiments were breaking and running.

One of his men turned, panicked, and tried to shoot his rifle to the rear, swearing desperately that the Rebels were creeping in behind them. Captain Holmes knocked him down with the flat of his sword and insisted that he was firing on his own men. Holmes quickly realized his own error when he heard another of his men scream, "The enemy *is* behind us!" When he turned to look, a Rebel bullet tore through Holmes's neck, sending him to the ground in half-conscious delirium.

Choking on his own blood, young Holmes listened as his regimental chaplain asked him, "You're a Christian, aren't you?" Holmes nodded weakly. "Well, then," the chaplain said, "That's all right"; he left the captain to die in God's hands.

Holmes passed out for the duration of the battle and, appearing dead, avoided capture. That night he stumbled to his feet and began wandering aimlessly among the piled corpses throughout the West Woods until a friend found him and tried to bandage his wounds. Able to generate a little humor even with a garish hole through both sides of his neck, he told his friend, "I'm glad this isn't a case for amputation for I have little confidence in your surgery."

Never losing that sense of humor, Oliver Wendell Holmes Jr. went on to serve for thirty years as a justice of the U.S. Supreme Court. Many of the opinions he wrote during his tenure were spiced with witticisms and remain legally relevant. Ironically, most of his decisions favored allowing the individual states to determine how to run their own court systems, a Southern-based, states' rights view against which he had fought during the Civil War.

The Unionists toppled in pain, desperation, panic, and death until their jumbled lines dissolved into smoke and a sticky-red mist.

For fifteen minutes, possibly less, the one-sided massacre raged on. Another Union soldier reported, "In less time than it takes to tell it, the ground was strewn with the bodies of the dead and wounded." When the Federals finally broke and ran, the Confederates charged in after them. The yipping Southerners pursued them up the hill, out of the woods, and into Miller's cornfield, slipping and sliding in the bloody muck beneath them.

The Rebels might have chased the Yankees all the way back to Washington had a Federal battery (or four to six artillery pieces) not rushed up to cover the Northern retreat. Double loads of Yankee cannister felled a great number of Rebels. By 10:00 A.M. the roaring in Miller's cornfield and the West Woods finally stopped.

Those whose ears had not been deafened by the four and a half hours of incessant bombast could hear moaning cries of anguish

The bodies of Rebel soldiers litter the fields surrounding Dunker Church. Once the fighting in Miller's cornfield and the West Woods ceased, more than eight thousand men were dead or wounded.

rising like swamp gas from every direction. More than eight thousand Americans lay dead or wounded after the worst fighting of the war to date. Despite all this sacrifice, the lines on the Confederate left and the Union right flanks stood exactly where they had been at dawn, and the battle was still not decided. Perhaps the conflict developing around an old, worn-down farm lane in the middle of Lee's line would prove more decisive. Certainly, it could prove no bloodier. Or could it?

CHAPTER FOUR

A Lane Made Bloody

General James Longstreet, commander of the right and center of the Confederate line, anxiously awaited the Yankee attack.

At 10:15 A.M. on September 17 the center of the Confederate line consisted of a half-mile long trench and the twenty-five hundred men who filled it. The trench itself was actually an eroded wagon path that had been worn down chest deep in some places. The soldiers were veterans of the South Mountain fight, the remains of General D. H. Hill's division. General James Longstreet commanded the overall Confederate right and center, and he was holding his only other division in reserve until he saw where the Yankees would be attacking next.

The barrel-chested, bearded Longstreet had already been out riding with Lee and Hill, trying to ascertain where the next attack would occur. Federal artillery had been taking potshots at the generals whenever they stopped, and one shot severed the forelegs of Hill's horse. Longstreet later wrote that when the hapless animal dropped to its shattered knees:

> Hill was in the most ludicrous position. With one foot in the stirrup, he made several efforts to get the other leg over the croup, but failed. Finally, we prevailed upon him to try the other end of the horse and he got down.

The men would laugh about the incident later, but for the time being they simply put the animal out of its misery and found Hill another mount.

Soon, they saw five thousand Yankees advancing toward the trench "with all the precision of a parade day waving banners above them that had apparently never been discolored by the smoke and dust of battle." The perfectly aligned Federals belonged to the division of General William French, an angry, moon-faced Mexican War veteran, now in charge of raw recruits.

Down in the Sunken Road, Colonel John B. Gordon's Georgians could not see beyond the rise one hundred yards to their front. They could hear the drums and bugles drawing closer, though, and the tin-cup clattering of Federal infantry. The feisty Colonel Gordon took an oath before General Lee, swearing, "My men are going to stay here, General, till the sun goes down or victory is won!" He would set the example, falling unconscious on the field with five separate bullet wounds. One of those bullets would slam directly into his handsome face, maiming him grotesquely for the rest of his life.

The Yankee drums grew louder, approaching from just beyond the rise to the front. Some of Gordon's troops admitted later that they wanted to get out of that trench before it became their final resting place. Running seemed to offer the only hope of escaping death, and a few actually tried to flee. But officers called "file-closers" stood behind the trench and held them in place with stinging slaps from their sabers.

Confederate colonel John B. Gordon bravely commanded his troops in the Sunken Road. This violent battle would be extremely devastating for Gordon, who incurred five bullet wounds and whose face was grotesquely maimed.

The Rebels crouched down and hid as best they could, becoming so quiet that their breathing was the only sound that could be heard. When the artillery fire stopped, a silence ensued as fearsome as the hottest of raging battles. Even as the flags of the first double-lined, blue wave appeared along the ridge just ahead of them, the Confederates kept their voices hushed. Some peered out to see the shoulder-to-shoulder wall of dark blue phantoms with their banners flying nobly, their bayoneted rifles shouldered straight up, and their posture menacingly erect.

After dressing up the lines by realigning the men shoulder to shoulder on the ridge, one thousand Federals (German-American immigrants who had never experienced battle) began their precisely measured descent toward the Sunken Road. The anxious Rebels shushed each other to be quiet until the blue lines were nearly on top of them. Then finally, at Colonel Gordon's command, they rose up as one and exploded hellfire and damnation into the Federal soldiers.

Instantly and horribly, the Federals fell to the ground, jerking and convulsing. "The effect was appalling," Colonel Gordon would write. "The entire front line, with few exceptions, went

Federal troops rallied under the spirited command of General Nathan Kimball. Unfortunately, Kimball's vigor could not overcome the Confederate assault and his troops were quickly laid to waste.

down in a consuming blast and brought down the enemy as grain falls before the reaper."

The second row, blinded by smoke, soon came down, too. Those who could run turned and did so, and some Yankees miraculously escaped. Little fight remained in them, however, and that which did drained away with the second and third Rebel volleys, leaving nothing of the German regiment but seven hundred mangled bodies sprawled out on the gentle rise and the fleeing backsides of the few survivors.

The Confederates in the trench rejoiced at the horror they had wrought, but their hugs and handshakes quickly subsided. They rapidly reloaded in preparation for the next assault and shoved their barrels through the stacked fence rails serving as the front of the breastwork.

The Yankees Keep Coming

On the Union side, General French's second Federal brigade came up on the low ridge in spite of the confused retreat of his first brigade. It returned the fire, silhouetted black against the bright blue sky, and listened to the Rebels' taunting jeers, "Go back there, you black devils!"

Terrified, French's recruits saw the Rebels on their right storm out of the Sunken Road in an attempt to take them by the flank. But they sighed as much relief as men under fire can sigh when Union artillery swept the Rebels from the field. However, the Confederates' ruthless firing and cursing whittled their ranks down to bloody shavings. Soon, the Northerners were stumbling over the gruesome dead at their feet and falling back to make way for the next Union brigade: Nathan Kimball's.

This fresh Yankee brigade was cheering at Kimball's repeated cry, "Now boys, we are going in, and we'll stay with them all day if they want us to!" But they didn't stay all day. In spite of pouring on a vigorous fire, they barely stayed half an hour before the Rebels in the trench laid them waste, too. One survivor said, "Our fighting before had been of the skirmishing sort. What we faced here was systematic killing."

By now, the green sloping meadow in front of the Sunken Road was carpeted with Federal blue, and the earth appeared to be crawling with the wounded and the soon-to-be dead as they wriggled and writhed in misery.

As a Union private wrote:

> Almost every blade of grass was moving. For some time I supposed that this was caused by the merry crickets; and it was not until I made a remark to that effect to one of our boys near me and noticed him laugh, that I knew that it was bullets that were falling thickly around us.

Sunken Road had not escaped the gore either. Confederates had been ripped open there in numbers just as ghastly as the Federal loss, and Southern blood was beginning to drain in dripping streams from the broken bodies. In the thunderous exchange, Confederates climbed about in the Sunken Road, crawling among the dead for cover. Bullets tore up the corpses and the ground around them as they crouched beneath the leaden whirlwind.

At about this time, Colonel Gordon collapsed with the wound to his face. He later wrote:

> I fell forward and lay unconscious with my face in my cap. I might have been smothered by the blood running from my wound but for the act of some Yankee, who at a previous hour in the battle, shot a hole through the cap, which let the blood out.

Bullets kept plowing through the trench and stripping the cornfield behind it. Men dropped. The bodies stacked up three and four deep. Blood was now seen flowing in rippled currents from beneath the grotesque pile.

General Longstreet, observing the battle from an artillery battery behind the trench, decided he had to act. He sent in the last of his fresh divisions, twenty-five hundred men under Richard Anderson, and they poured into the Bloody Lane just in time to face a second Federal division commanded by the hard-driving Israel Richardson.

Thousands of Confederate and Union soldiers repose in Bloody Lane, the gruesome half-mile long trench that became a mass grave during the Battle of Antietam.

The famed Irish brigade came charging down first, its emerald flag fluttering with shamrocks and a golden harp. These men were immigrants from Catholic Ireland, and their priest rode into battle with them. Prancing back and forth before their lines, the father administered conditional absolution, last rites, for those about to die. Thus prepared, these battle-crazed Celtic warriors shot and yelled, cursed and scrapped, raising the pitch of the struggle to an even louder, more lacerating plane.

A recruitment flyer invites able-bodied men to join the third Irish regiment and to "carry the American Eagle over the Potomac, down like an avalanche through the land of Dixie, emulating the Glory of the other Irish Regiments."

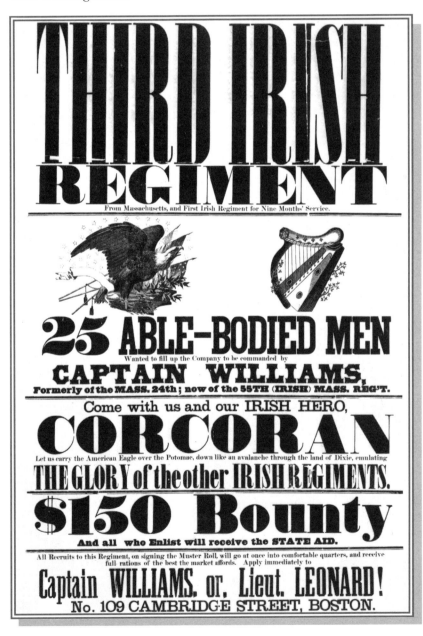

The Luck of the Irish

To say that General Thomas Francis Meagher (pronounced Mayor) led a colorful life is like saying that a little blood was shed at Antietam. Born and raised in Ireland, he was a fighting revolutionary by the age of eighteen, battling to free his beloved homeland from England.

The British captured and imprisoned him on the isolated island of Tasmania. After three years of captivity, the fiery redhead escaped to America and began fighting for Irish independence from the tenements of New York City.

He raised money, gave speeches, and eventually formed a brigade of Irish immigrants ostensibly for service in the U.S. Army. His dream all along, though, was to season his men in this little American war for ultimate service in Ireland.

He never could have realized just how costly the war here would become and how completely it would consume his dream brigade. At Antietam alone, he lost nearly half his men. Fredericksburg, three months later, would claim the other half.

While his Irish Brigade fought, it garnered the accolades of the entire army (in spite of the prejudice against them because they were Roman Catholics). Perhaps they had to scrap harder to prove their worth to the American descendants of Englishmen, or perhaps they were born, like their Celtic ancestors, to be fearless warriors.

At least part of General Meagher's courage, though, seemed to come from a bottle of whiskey (a reputation all the Irishmen had to live down). When he claimed that his horse had been shot out from under him at Bloody Lane, an unadmiring colonel wrote, "Meagher was drunk, and fell from that horse."

After losing his brigade, he was transferred to the west where his temper, politics, and drinking caused him further problems. He was serving as the acting governor of the Montana territory in 1867 (still scheming ways to lead Irish-American troops back to Ireland) when he fell, dead drunk, from a riverboat and drowned.

One observer remembered the attack this way:

On the great field were riderless horses and scattering men, clouds of dirt from solid shot and exploding shells, long dark lines of infantry swaying to and fro, with columns of smoke rising from their muskets and white puffs from the batteries. The sun shone brightly on all this scene of tumult, this savage continual thunder that cannot compare to any sound I have ever heard.

But for all the "impetuosity and recklessness of Irish soldiers in the charge" and the shouts of their flamboyant commander, "Boys raise the colors and follow me!" the Irish brigade's assault broke up like all the others though not before causing serious damage to the Confederate right flank.

Lessons Learned

Confederate General Daniel Harvey Hill taught mathematics before the war and wrote several math textbooks from a distinctively Southern perspective, which he aptly called "the Southern Series." This grumbling, irritable, intensely religious man could find no place in his Christian heart for tolerance, especially for the "vile, damned, Yankees" he had grown to hate so vehemently over the years.

Attempting to teach his brand of morality as well as the principles of mathematics, he used examples based upon what he called "Yankee cunning." For example, Hill wrote, "A Yankee mixes a certain quantity of wooden (fake) nutmegs, which cost him one-fourth cent apiece, with a quantity of real nutmegs, worth four cents apiece" and asked how much the Yankee would be cheating the buyer if he sold him this or that many.

In another instance, Hill began a problem by stating: "The field at the Battle of Buena Vista (in the Mexican War) is six and a half miles from Saltillo. Two Indiana volunteers ran away from the field of battle at the same time." He then asked how long would it take the Yankee cowards to get to the rear if they ran at various speeds.

Whether or not Hill's students learned any math from his texts is unknown. It is safe to assume, however, that the young minds that solved his problems went on to become ardent haters of "Yankee cunning" and fierce soldiers when the time came to apply their math lessons to the battlefield.

The Rebels on the right flank belonged to Anderson's newly arrived division, and they were proving to be less steady than D. H. Hill's men. They would have to rally and rally fast. Already most of their officers and file-closers had either died or cowered into the trench. This wickedly smothering din had lapsed beyond anyone's control; still the courageous and the petrified remained in place.

They held the trench, ducking and shooting, until the last of the Irish brigade had advanced and receded in its turn. They took advantage of the brief lull that followed to stack corpses for cover and bandage their own bleeding wounds.

The lull did not last long. The second of Israel Richardson's brigades came over the rise with that belligerent division commander personally leading the way. He was swearing floridly and swinging his saber, doing the job Brigadier General John Caldwell should have been doing. Just a few minutes earlier, "Fighting Dick" had found Caldwell trying to hide behind a haystack, and Richardson had quickly and profanely relieved Caldwell of brigade command. Now, face blackened with powder and throat raw from shouting, "Goddamn the field officers," the fierce-eyed Richardson drove Caldwell's brigade ahead by himself.

Richardson's Yankees charged and fell, fired and died. Hill's Rebels did the same—until the Sunken Road was clogged with butternut bodies and the slope was piled high with blue ones. Both sides wearied, their dead drained white, but neither showed signs of giving up. Each line stood firm against the other and slugged it out through the grinding minutes. More than fifteen thousand men now grappled in this close-quartered fray like cats with their tails tied together.

Cannon blew holes in the ranks and spewed victims high into the air while the ceaseless musketry hacked men down like cordwood. At the height of the maelstrom, one man fell every two seconds only to be stepped over or used for cover. Remarkably, the noise and the bombast, the savagery, and the fire did not seem to lessen in the absence of the fallen soldiers.

A few Rebels eventually did give up the fight, creeping over the mire of corpses to flee. Their shocked eyes had seen enough; their instincts to survive had won out. They had done their part for over two hours amid the death and the sizzling heat. They certainly must have figured that it was someone else's turn to carry on the fight. Many Rebels probably did not realize that there simply was no one else left. However, that was not the case for the Yankees.

The Union colonel of a fresh regiment said:

> The shouts of our men and their sudden dash toward the sunken road, so startled the enemy that their fire visibly slackened, their line wavered, and squads of two and three began leaving the road and running into the corn behind it.

The fighting was not yet over, but its ending had at last begun.

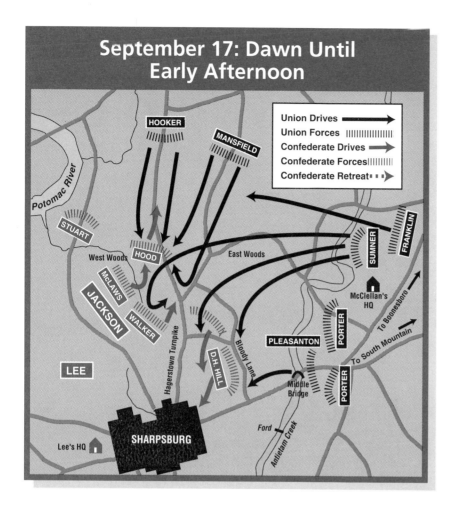

September 17: Dawn Until Early Afternoon

Legend:
- Union Drives ➡
- Union Forces |||||||||||||||
- Confederate Drives ➡
- Confederate Forces||||||||||
- Confederate Retreat ▪▪▪▶

HOOKER

MANSFIELD

Potomac River

STUART

West Woods — HOOD

East Woods

FRANKLIN

SUMNER

McClellan's HQ

To Boonesboro

McLAWS

JACKSON

WALKER

Hagerstown Turnpike

PORTER

PLEASANTON

To South Mountain

D.H. HILL

Bloody Lane

LEE

Middle Bridge

PORTER

Ford

Lee's HQ

SHARPSBURG

Antietam Creek

The Confederate Center Breaks

There was still plenty of killing and maiming being suffered throughout the Federal force but not enough to prevent the Northern army from gaining the momentum necessary to breach the Confederate trench. General Richardson called for his last brigade, commanded by Colonel Francis Barlow, and it attacked the extreme Rebel right from the high ground on that side.

"The minnie balls, shot and shell rained down on us from every direction except the rear," a Confederate sergeant wrote. "Many men took this chance to leave the field entirely. Many officers were killed and wounded." Amid the pandemonium of shells, screams, and rifle fire, the Rebels responded by trying to wheel their right flank around to face the enemy that was now pouring its fusillade of lead lengthwise up the trench.

The trench that had served the Southerners for three hours as a protective breastwork suddenly became an open grave. In the middle of the trench, they thought that the men on the right flank were caving in instead of repositioning themselves to continue the fight. Panic seized the entire Southern force, causing a

A Civil War era photograph depicts the aftermath of Bloody Lane. The trench, which had protected the Southerners during the onset of the battle, was filled with dead soldiers after the battle ceased.

dozen men to run—then two dozen and then three—until the entire trench emptied out. One Rebel reported, "The slaughter was terrible! I could scarcely extricate myself from the dead and wounded around me. We had to either run or surrender; we ran rapidly!"

Richardson's Yankees pursued. General French's men occupied the Bloody Lane and kneeled down upon "that ghastly flooring" to fire. A Northern journalist wrote:

Ah, what a crash! A white cloud, gleams of lightning, a yell, a hurrah, and then up in the cornfield a great commotion, men firing into each other's faces, the Confederate line breaking, the ground strewn with prostrate forms!

The Confederate center was splitting wide open. Soon the battle would be lost. In forlorn hope, Longstreet threw in the absolute last that he had: five hundred men on each crumbling flank and a few cannon in the middle. Longstreet's staff had to man one of the abandoned guns (its crew were all dead) while he held their horses. They managed to slow down the approaching Federals with a few blasts of cannister, but "Old Pete" knew his staff could not hold the Federals long.

The pitiful, though admirable, Confederate attack on the left stalled into a stand-up rifle fight at close range. Before long, overwhelming Federal force cut scores of the Rebels down and drove the rest back in disarray. On the right, "General Hill, in a clear, loud voice gave the order 'ATTENTION! CHARGE!'"; he personally led five hundred stragglers as they threw themselves defiantly back at the Yankee horde "in line of battle yelling awfully."

The two hopeless charges were dispersed, but they bought enough time for the Confederates to assemble twenty field artillery pieces from all over the smoking battlefield. Stonewall Jackson found an inactive battery of six guns and inquired sternly as to why they were not helping out in the middle. The battery commander replied, "No orders and no support." Jackson made short work of the man, ordering him to "Go in at once! You artillery men are too afraid of losing your guns!"

The miscellaneous cannon opened up from high ground to the left and rear of Longstreet's little battery. The iron shower put

During the Civil War, cannons wreaked havoc on advancing troops, quickly cutting men down with their explosive volleys.

an end to the Yankee pursuit, at least for the time being. Richardson ordered his Federals to fall back and regroup, fully expecting reinforcements from McClellan. While he waited, he was mortally wounded by a cannon blast, but at least he was satisfied that the reserve troops would make his sacrifice and that of his division worth the cost in pain and blood.

But Little Mac did not send them. After having used two divisions in the middle of the battle already, McClellan decided not to risk throwing in more troops, even though the Confederates had apparently been swept from the field. Once again, he refused to commit any of his thirty thousand reserves, squandering another hard-won opportunity to win the battle.

By 1:00 P.M. the fight at the Sunken Road had ground down to an ear-ringing silence. Through the murmur of low moans and whimpers, guns and rifles could be heard intensifying to the south, but few paid any attention. Their senses were overloaded by the six thousand casualties carpeting the fields and overflowing Bloody Lane. There could not be much of a scrap brewing down there anyway, many thought. Wasn't everybody dead or wounded by now?

CHAPTER FIVE

Burnside's Bridge and Beyond

Since 9:00 A.M. on September 17 General McClellan had been urging his old friend Ambrose Burnside to cross Antietam Creek on the Union left flank and attack the village of Sharpsburg from the south. But each messenger that McClellan sent to set a fire under General Burnside returned with the same observation: Despite his eleven thousand men and fifty cannon, the bald, mutton-chopped corps commander was dawdling.

He also appeared to be sulking, the couriers said, perhaps because his old friend McClellan had transferred away a sizable portion of his Ninth Corps and given it to Joseph Hooker on the north end of the battlefield. Others said that Burnside was determined to cross a gray, stone, triple-arch bridge where Confederate strength was greatest instead of wading across the lightly defended fords above and below it.

Whatever the cause, the effect was the same. Burnside was stalled before the bridge, and so were his men. Instead of being at full alert and ready to move, one Massachusetts soldier wrote that "the whirring of the shells above us had a drowsing effect, and some of our men dozed." Others enjoyed a routine mail call and wandered off among the trees to read their letters.

Most idled, stood, milled, and lounged about uselessly on the high ground above the stone bridge listening to the rifle cracks of skirmishing and sniping down below them. The wounded from the little valley were arriving steadily by whatever means they could manage, adding misery to the muddle. It was, however, the uncommitted, apparently leaderless men clumped so loosely together who had this hill and the Union advance most mired.

Despite orders to cross Antietam Creek and capture Sharpsburg, General Ambrose Burnside sluggishly waited for the opportunity to cross the heavily fortified bridge.

Marylanders evacuate Sharpsburg as tensions mount between Union and Confederate forces.

General McClellan was growing impatient and strengthened the tone of his dispatches to Burnside. He called after one departing courier, "Tell him [Burnside] if it costs 10,000 men, he must go now!" At last, the inactive Ninth Corps commander began to stir enough to send a few regiments down the hill and into battle.

They quickly bogged down, however, or got lost or were beaten back by rifle fire, convincing Burnside even more completely that the enemy had a massive force dug into the forested bluff on the other side. One of his officers called the Confederate position "virtually impregnable to a direct attack over the bridge." So General Burnside ground his operations to a halt again, wringing his hands over the assumed Rebel strength.

The Confederate Bluff

If only Burnside had known the true size and condition of the Confederate right flank, he might have reacted differently. General Lee had already stripped it down to a skeletal force in order to reinforce his left and center (Miller's cornfield and Bloody Lane). No more than four hundred men remained to defend the bluffs above the bridge. There were hardly any men at the fords. But these rapid-loading Georgians were managing to pour out a wholesale fire with the few rifles they had at their disposal.

The bluff from which most were firing rose one hundred feet over the span. Tall oak trees offered Southern sharpshooters further elevation from which to do their deadly work. Abandoned quarries carved into the slope provided ready-made breastworks, and the men had dug a maze of trenches that were ideal vantage points for shooting down upon the enemy.

Brigadier General Robert Toombs commanded this meager yet determined force of Southerners. A gruff, surly, angry-eyed man, Toombs was a career politician who had lately served as the Confederacy's secretary of state. He coveted the Confederate presidency, though, and believed that he would be propelled into that office by joining the army and winning a great military victory. "The day after such an event," he had written, "I will retire, if I live through it."

Burnside Stirs at Last

At the pointed urging of several high-ranking officers personally sent by General McClellan, Burnside began to give the ambitious Toombs his opportunity for triumph. This time, the blundering Burnside ordered two regiments to run in column, or four abreast in a long line, directly for the entrance to the bridge.

The colonel leading the hopeless assault saw his regiments "shrinking and elbowing out under this tremendous fire and just ready to break." He demanded, "What in the hell are you doing there? Straighten that line there! Forward!" But the colonel's men turned and ran, after being torn apart by the fusillade of bullets from the smoking trees.

Colonel Edward Ferrero led the charge to cross Burnside's bridge and confront the enemy.

Again, General Burnside paused, wracked by indecision. The sight of his bloodied men streaming to the rear seemed to immobilize him further. A friend remarked, "He shrank from his responsibility with sincere modesty."

By 1:00 P.M. the action on the rest of the battlefield had stopped. McClellan, needlessly concerned about the possibility of a massive Confederate counterattack, locked all of his men into defensive positions except for those at Burnside's bridge, and again he prodded his friend.

General Burnside reluctantly obeyed, ordering in the two most aggressive regiments of his beloved Ninth Corps, the Fifty-first Pennsylvania and the Fifty-first New York. Their commander, former dance instructor Colonel Edward Ferrero, called out to the assembled one thousand men, "It is General Burnside's special request that the two 51sts take that bridge! Will you do it?"

Expecting a rousing reply, Ferrero was disappointed when he did not get it. Instead, a corporal speaking for the rest grumbled back, "Will you give us our whiskey,

So Disgraceful a Wound

Many participants in the last hours of the battle witnessed an unusual sight. Survivors even regarded it later as a humorous one. Droves of Confederates fleeing for their lives were running backwards as fast as their back-pedaling legs could move them. They were not doing so in order to continue firing or to keep an eye on the pursuing enemy's movements and certainly not to facilitate an orderly withdrawal.

One Virginia private summed up the situation like this: "I was afraid of being struck in the back and I turned around in running so as to avoid if possible so disgraceful a wound. I at least managed to not to come out ahead in this race."

The chasing Yankees laughed and jeered at the Rebels as if they were winning in some school-yard game. But many of them ended up doing their own retreating before the day ended, and there is no record of their being ashamed enough of their own cowardice to even worry about where bullets might strike them.

Colonel, if we take it?" (They had lost their ration as a disciplinary measure.)

"Yes, by God!" the dapper little colonel bellowed. "You shall have as much as you want!" Now he got the rousing cheer he had been looking for, and he prepared to lead the battle.

The two regiments lined up in a road just south of the bridge. They were hidden from the Rebels there but would have to dash across three hundred yards of open space to make it to the mouth of the bridge.

They poured down off the hill in a column of fours and stormed along the creek toward the bridge. The Rebel fire from the bluff intensified, and dozens of Yankees fell in the screaming surge forward. Out in the uncovered stretch, they sprinted like bears, shouting and cursing, pushing and stumbling, shooting when they got the chance.

The two fresh regiments roared past the wreckage of those sent before, heartened by the cheers from the pinned-down survivors. More and more Yankees dropped from the splintering shells and musketry, but the others pressed on. Sword-swinging officers drove the column forward, shouting until they were red faced and hoarse. Color, or flag, bearers led the way, waving their flags in the smoky air.

The Confederate fire kept Ferrero's men from making it all the way to the bridge, but they fanned out along walls and fences on either side of its entrance. "We were then ordered to halt and commence firing," wrote a Union lieutenant, "and the way we showered the lead across that creek was nobody's business!"

On the Rebel side, a Georgia colonel observed, "The combined fire of Federal infantry and artillery was terrific." Dead men fell from the trees as if a giant had shaken them out. Soldiers exhausted from three hours of fighting began to break out and run back up the hill toward Sharpsburg. But the reckless and the brave remained.

One of the Union regimental colonels waved his hat and shouted with a raspy voice, "Come on, boys, for I can't halloo anymore!" And he motioned for his men to charge onto the bridge.

One inspired Yankee captain ran out onto the fieldstone span and exposed himself to intense fire. A sergeant followed, then the flag bearers, and suddenly, a gallant rush was on.

The men swarmed into each other, charging headlong onto the narrow bridge, and took fearsome casualties along the way. One Unionist later recalled that before they could even get to the other side, "the enemy deserted their works and scattered over the hills like a drove of scared sheep."

Jumping over the bodies of those who dropped in front of them, the Federals fought their way across the bridge and hounded the fleeing Confederates with howls every bit as fierce as any rebel yell. The Southerners fired back on the run, though, and Union casualties continued to mount.

The Union flag gallantly leads the Yankees across Antietam Creek and into battle with the fleeing Rebels.

Slipping and sliding on the blood-slickened stones, hundreds more Federals poured over the creek. They quickly swept up the bluff side, capturing or killing the last of the Rebels with bayonets, bullets, and raw-nerved courage.

Another Crucial Delay

Every Southerner with legs and sense was retreating by this time. Some stopped halfway up the hill to support a twelve-gun battery. The rest headed for the last lines at Sharpsburg, and what they found when they got there shocked even the most hardened among them. Fewer than fifteen hundred men stood ready to meet the final Union assault.

Stonewall Jackson ordered a boy to shinny up a tree and report down on enemy strength. "How many troops are over there," Jackson inquired.

"Who-e-e!" the boy replied. "There are oceans of them, General!"

"Count the flags, sir," Stonewall said firmly, and when the boy reached thirty-nine, Jackson droned, "That will do, come down, sir."

Facing ten thousand attackers, General Lee had his officers round up every spare man and artillery piece and throw them into line on the ridge running south of Sharpsburg. They corralled any man still on his feet into the tattered line: the shell-shocked, the exhausted, staff men, musicians, teamsters, stragglers, and cooks. The general's officers had no trouble finding rifles. There was a surplus in the hands of the dead.

And there they stood, the last remnants of the Confederate army. There were no more men left to send in. Death seemed certain now, and these haggard men who seemed resigned to their fate began to say their last prayers. The only hope was that General A. P. Hill and his three thousand men might somehow arrive from Harpers Ferry, but no one was counting on miracles at this point. Besides, Hill was still at least two hours away.

The Southerners stood their ground nonetheless, waiting for their turn to die, too proud or too tired or too depressed to run. They watched for Federals coming up the cleared hill. Palms sweating, ears ringing, and mouths caked dry with sulfured gunpowder, they waited and waited but the Yankees did not come. They waited nearly two scorching hours in the afternoon sun, and still no Yankees appeared.

The End Finally Comes

At the bottom of the hill, the Unionists had been lying paralyzed by the very numbers that made them strong. If Burnside had not had eight thousand fresh troops about a mile back in his rear, he would have struck forth immediately with the men who had

He Also Served . . .

Not every hero at the Battle of Antietam carried a rifle and a bayonet. There was at least one, a twenty-four-year-old sergeant from Ohio who earned a field promotion in a completely different way. He risked his life in order to provide the men in his regiment with the one thing they wanted most. It was not ammunition or powder, cannonballs or percussion caps, rifles or horses or guns. No, it was coffee. Pure and simple, hot and black, to lift their sagging spirits.

Serving as the Twenty-third Ohio's commissary sergeant, he was not required to leave the rear area, but he took it upon himself to rush his commissary wagon all the way down to Burnside's bridge during the worst of the fighting. Time and time again, the young sergeant crawled under fierce Confederate fire to deliver his rejuvenating elixir to the exhausted and famished Union soldiers.

The coffee seemed to work its magic, and the Federals eventually rallied and took the bridge. However, A. P. Hill arrived with his own brand of Rebel stimulation and drove the Federals back down. This commissary sergeant worked above and beyond the call

During the Battle of Antietam, William McKinley risked his life attending to the needs of his fellow soldiers.

of duty for the rest of the night, serving the many hundreds who came to him for relief. His name? William McKinley, the man who would become the twenty-fifth president of the United States.

---

taken the bridge. However, he wasted two crucial hours squeezing the reinforcements across the span without even bothering to use the fords. At 3:00 P.M., though, he began driving them up the hill and they came on like an irresistible force.

A Rebel directly in front of Burnside's three-quarter-mile swath recalled:

> The first thing we saw appear was the gilt eagle that surmounted the pole, then the top of the flag, next the flutter of the Stars and Stripes; then their hats came in sight; still rising, the faces emerged; next a range of curious eyes appeared, then such a hurrah as only the Yankee troops could give broke the stillness, and they surged toward us.

The Confederates were outnumbered but put up a valiant fight and suffered many gruesome wounds. However, they could not stop the endless rush of Yankees on the left of the line, and many Rebels began to fall back to the village. The conflagration there, however, rivaled anything on the battlefield; the throng of panicked soldiers jamming the street, clawing desperately to escape the onslaught, seized many with a new horror.

Shells were bursting up and down the flaming thoroughfare, blowing men and animals apart. Maddened mules bucked against ambulances that were draining streams of blood through the floorboards to the dirt street. One hysterical slave woman, seeing the blood splattering down, screamed, "Oh, Lord! Oh, Lord! Oh, Lord!" until the ambulances passed. Her hoarse voice gave out at about the same time.

Even the pigeon flocks in the sky were swarming in confused circles over the gnashing mob as the artillery blasted plaster from churches and houses. A Confederate surgeon who

As the Yankees pursued the Rebels through the streets of Sharpsburg, artillery blasts marred the plaster on this Lutheran church.

September 17: Afternoon

SHARPSBURG

Lee's HQ

To Shepherdstown

LONGSTREET

BURNSIDE

Burnside's Bridge

Ford

Ford

Ford

A.P. HILL

From Harpers Ferry

McCLELLAN

Hagerstown Turnpike

Antietam Creek

Potomac River

Boteler's Ford

Union Drives	➤
Union Forces	||||||||||||||
Confederate Drives	➤
Confederate Forces	|||||||

survived the cataclysm later wrote, "I was never so tired of shelling in my life. I hate cannons!"

The Yankees on the Rebel right sensed impending victory, too, and let down their guard as a result. They were facing little opposition and supposed that their part of the battle was already won.

They were wrong. Off to the south, two long columns of infantry approached. The dust cloud they made obscured the colors of their uniforms. From a knoll behind the battlefield, General Lee pointed wearily to the column on the left and asked an officer with a telescope, "What troops are those, sir?"

The officer squinted into the scope and said with disappointment, "They are flying the United States flag, General."

Lee pointed to the dust cloud on the right and asked, "What about them?"

The officer turned his glass to the right after studying that column for a painfully long time, he broke out in a grin and cried, "They are flying the Virginia and Confederate flags, sir!"

Sighing, General Lee said with as much emotion as he could manage, "It is A. P. Hill from Harpers Ferry."

And indeed it was. Soon, Hill's division attacked without wasting the time to come on line properly. The resulting whirlwind of charging Confederate riflemen opened up on the unsuspecting Yankee flank and scythed them down like hay. The shocked Federal survivors could not maneuver in time to face Hill's men. Attempting to wheel left under the fire, they fell apart and ran.

A Small Town's Terror

Most of Sharpsburg, Maryland's, twenty-five hundred residents supported the cause of the Union. That allegiance made the destruction of their pleasant community all the more disturbing to them. After all, Yankee guns had fired the cannonballs into their homes from the beginning of the day until the end, and Yankee cannonballs drove them to their cellars and set their homes ablaze.

For twelve hours, the cowering inmates of those improvised bomb shelters endured the most terrifying of all wartime horrors: the anxious, fearful, razor-edged anticipation of where the next shell would hit. Each time a shell did hit, the pent-up fright caused by its whistling descent burst out of them into panic. "Every time the firing began extra hard," one woman said, "the babies would cry and the dogs would bark, and some of the aged would break out in prayer."

Perhaps the prayers had some effect, for civilian injuries were surprisingly low. The shelling in the streets flipped many Rebel stragglers "over and over like a wagon wheel," and several others were bowled into eternity by iron balls skittering along the cobblestones. Only one civilian, a young girl, lost her life during the bombardment. It is likely, however, that her death seemed a massacre to the loved ones in whose arms she died.

It would have been bad enough if they had run straight back down the hill, but they went sideways, which caused the regimental formations next to them to collapse into each other like so many dominoes. In less than an hour, the Federals who had been so close to winning the flank and the battle were in full, confused retreat. General Burnside sent a desperate dispatch to McClellan for reserves, but he got the same old refrain from the Young Napoleon, "I can do no more. I have no infantry."

Thus, the battle ended with the lines drawn almost exactly where they had stood at dawn. The only differences now were how thin those lines had become and how many dead and dying men separated them. The Federals could have won the battle with one more concerted push at any point on the field, but that push never came. General Lee, risking everything, held his ground as the sun started down. General McClellan, risking nothing, did the same.

CHAPTER SIX

Aftermath

s the fighting was winding down, one Rebel boy remembered, "The sun seemed almost to go backwards in the sky. It appeared as if night would never come." Night did come though, silencing the nervous rifle fire that had been crackling up and down the lines since dusk. Sounds far more terrifying than those, however, soon crowded the silence and filled it even more disturbingly: the cries and moans of young Americans dying from the crusty-red wounds of war.

Men on both sides groped for missing friends amid the hellish chorus of sobs. "I squinted," said one, "holding my lantern closer, but I could not see much at first." When he rubbed his eyes and strained to look into the shadowed, smoky murk, he could make

Dead soldiers were found scattered across Hagerstown Road (pictured), near Sharpsburg, following the brutal Battle of Antietam.

out far more than he cared to. The man recalled, "I fell to my knees and gagged, sickened by the ghastly scene."

It had been bad enough for the soldiers to see the gore during the heat of battle when the stresses and strains of trying to survive kept them focused on other things (the enemy, finding cover, loading and reloading). But when freed from direct threats to their own lives, it was impossible to ignore the carnage.

An aide to Stonewall Jackson wrote:

> The pitiable pleas for water and appeals for help were much more horrible to listen to than the deadliest sounds of battle. Silent were the dead, and motionless. But here and there were raised stiffened arms; heads made a last effort to raise themselves from the ground; prayers were mingled with oaths, the oaths of delirium; men were wriggling over the earth; and midnight hid all distinction between the blue and the gray.

My horse trembled under me in terror, looking down at the ground, sniffing the scent of blood, stepping falteringly as a horse will over or by the side of human flesh; afraid to stand still, hesitating to go on, his animal instinct shuddered at this cruel human mystery. Once his foot slid into a little shallow filled with blood and spurted a little stream on his leg and my boot. I had had a surfeit of blood that day and I couldn't stand this. I dismounted and, giving the reins to my courier, I started on foot into the wood of Dunker Church.

(Below, right) While doctors at a field hospital care for wounded soldiers, those who could not be saved were gathered for burial (below).

The situation was no better there, though, or at any other location within ten miles of the battlefield. Since early morning, the entire area had been converted into one vast field hospital. Lanterns now burned in doors and windows, and the screams of amputees (conscious because there was no chloroform) lashed through the moon-silvered darkness. There were screams when the knives cut down to the bone and when the hacksaws started grinding back and forth. The screams crescendoed when the connective flesh had to be scissored away and dissolved into anguished semiconscious moans as the surgeon cried, "Next!"

Piles of discarded limbs stood head high among the hundreds awaiting their turn. Feet still had their toes and hands had their fingernails, but the lumps of fat-marbled flesh bore no resemblance to anything that could be identified by name. The only beneficiaries of this medieval grotesquerie were the billions of flies.

A local woman whose home had been converted to a hospital wrote of the Confederate wounded:

> They filled every building and overflowed into the country round, into farm-houses, barns, corn-cribs, cabins,—wherever four walls and a roof were found together. Those able to travel were sent on to Winchester and other towns back from the river, but their departure seemed to make no appreciable difference.

The next morning, Thursday, September 18, did not improve the sights or the sounds, and the burning sun created yet another misery: the sulfurized putrid odor of human flesh beginning to rot. One Union officer said of the bodies, "Many were as black as Negroes. Their heads and faces were hideously swelled, covered with dust until they looked like clods." A Federal general ordered some of the corpses burned but countermanded his order when "this made the stench only increase in volume."

A Time to Heal

Survivors on both sides made attempts to recover their wounded and bury their dead, but they did not want to risk being shot by snipers. At various times and places along the lines, the Rebels and Yankees agreed to brief truces in order to tend the stricken, and the irony of the situation did not escape one Confederate. He wrote, "It seemed very curious to see men on both sides come together and talk to each other when the day before we were firing at each other." A Yankee watching Confederates struggle to reach his side for aid wrote: "They were wounded in all imaginable ways and crying piteously for help. One poor fellow had one leg shot off and was hobbling along with two guns for crutches."

For all their well-intentioned efforts, though, it was simply impossible for the stretcher bearers (who were musicians when not assigned this grisly duty) and other concerned soldiers to recover

America's Bloodiest Day: The Final Tally

September 17, 1862, still stands as the bloodiest single day in American history—but just what does that mean? How many Americans fell in that fourteen-hour maelstrom as compared with other similar tragedies?

Records show that more casualties were inflicted at the Battle of Antietam than in the French and Indian War, the War of 1812, and the Mexican War combined and nearly as many as during the entire seven years of the Revolutionary War. Neither D day, Pearl Harbor, nor Iwo Jima during World War II claimed greater American losses, and it took six months of the worst fighting in Vietnam to match the cost of that one late-summer day in 1862.

But statistics alone do not begin to reflect the true terror of Antietam—the magnitude and intensity of the personal suffering and pain it caused. Men, not numbers, lost their arms and legs that day. Families, not statistics, lost their husbands and fathers.

Afterward, it was real farms that failed and real businesses that went bankrupt because of the physical and mental disabilities the battle caused. Loved ones would never be able to fully understand their veterans or the wet-eyed silences that overtook them each time the "glorious" struggle was mentioned.

Each one of the numbers adding up to the 23,582 killed and wounded men represents a body maimed or destroyed, the effects of which rippled out far beyond the pools of blood that gathered on the battlefield. Spiritual and emotional life blood was spilled as well. Perhaps therein lies the deeper justification for the Battle of Antietam's being called "America's Bloodiest Day," for blood can be shed in many forms from wounds both hidden and seen.

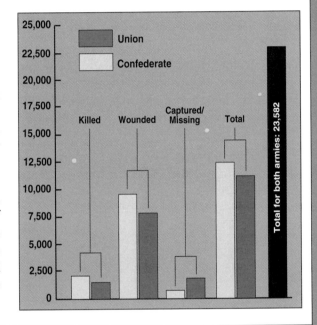

the many casualties during the short cease-fires. After all, some seventeen thousand men had been cut down, and some were still clinging to life in the fields and woods.

Even when the injured could be carted from the field, there were woefully few people to nurse them. The army surgeons and orderlies did all that they could, but they needed help. One Massachusetts woman, a clerk in the U.S. Patent Office, was one of the civilians to lend a hand. Early in the war she had raised money to buy sorely needed medical supplies that she distributed to those suffering in hospitals.

She eventually quit her job in Washington, D.C., and obtained permission to travel with the Union army. Driving her own wagon crammed full with the medicine and supplies she had gathered, this determined woman set out to see her first real battle: Antietam. The army surgeons expected her to faint and flee, but they did not know her courage (though soon the whole world would). She nursed the wounded right at the front—so close, in fact, that a bullet ripped through her sleeve and killed a man she was treating.

This brave woman continued her nursing and supply gathering throughout the war, establishing relief operations along the way. She pioneered the first efficient means of determining the status of those missing in action, a service that became invaluable to waiting families. In 1881, however, she made a contribution to all the people of the country. Using experience gained during the Civil War, she turned her talents toward helping average citizens devastated by civilian emergencies. She called her relief agency the American Red Cross, and it is thriving yet today. The woman was Clara Barton, the angel of the battlefield.

(Above, left) During the Civil War, civilians were called upon to nurse the wounded in field hospitals. Clara Barton (pictured), perhaps the most courageous of all volunteers, traveled with the Union army, nursing wounded soldiers and providing medical supplies.

Lee Risks Everything

In spite of all the efforts directed toward the casualties at Antietam, ninety-five thousand survivors remained and commanders on both sides seemed unsure about what to do with them. As always, there were three options: attack, flee, or defend. The latter option allowed each commander a little time before having to make any more far-reaching decisions, and accordingly, both Lee and McClellan ordered their men to dig in.

Confederate general Robert E. Lee resolved to defend his position at Antietam, although greatly outnumbered by the Yankees.

General Lee was definitely taking the greater chance. He could count upon no more than thirty thousand men (including five thousand newly arrived stragglers from Harpers Ferry). He was overwhelmingly outnumbered, but he was accustomed to that disadvantage, and he had other, better reasons to stay.

For one thing, Lee's men needed rest. They were suffering from a leaden exhaustion brought on by hundreds of miles marched and thousands of bullets dodged. They also needed food, which a day's rest might allow them to forage, and ammunition, which they could scavenge from the dead.

As in other battles, General Lee refused to leave the wounded behind. He wanted to remain at Sharpsburg long enough to transport the wounded back into Virginia where they might have a chance to heal and fight again.

He also wanted to give the men in Harpers Ferry enough time to transport the captured Union guns and equipment farther south. Lee had two more subtle, but highly compelling, reasons for ordering his army to remain in place: his poor opinion of McClellan's generalship and his concern for the morale of his own troops.

The previous day, General Lee had watched his opponent squander several opportunities to crush the Southern forces, and Lee saw no reason why McClellan would suddenly become aggressive this second day and risk an attack. Lee also refused to give his Army of Northern Virginia the impression that they had been defeated after fighting so hard and sacrificing so much when, in fact, the battle had been fought to a draw. So he took perhaps his greatest gamble of the entire Maryland campaign and kept his beleaguered army defiantly in place.

The Angels of Shepherdstown

After the fight, some seventeen thousand wounded men sought relief in the villages near the battlefield. The one thousand residents of Shepherdstown, Virginia, just across the Potomac from Sharpsburg, committed every church, house, and outbuilding to the care, feeding, and nursing of nearly five thousand Confederate casualties. That meant that every home in town gave its beds and floors to an average of ten (and as many as thirty) bloody, smelly, filthy soldiers.

Several young belles kept diaries of their participation in those awesome events. One wrote:

> Our cook rushed into the house. She had seen wagons coming up the hill full of wounded men and, measuring to her shoulder on her outstretched arm, she said, "The blood was running out of them that deep!" We set bravely to work and washed away the blood or stanched it as best we could. But what did we know of wounds beyond a cut finger or a boil?

Another girl running out into the same hellish scene recorded:

> I saw my first wounded man with two soldiers supporting him as the surgeon probed for a ball in his wrist. He asked for water and I ran to get some and then fanned him while the cutting and probing continued. No anesthetic relieved his pain and no cry escaped his lips, save once in a while a long breath and an "ouch." At last the ball was cut out. He never flinched or fainted. But I nearly did.

Another young woman recalled:

> We worked right on the streets and sidewalks to comfort the men as more hospitals were created. There were noise, dust, confusion, throngs of stragglers, horsemen galloping about, teamsters swearing, wagons groaning, in the midst of which men were dying, fresh wounded arriving, surgeons amputating limbs and dressing wounds, women going in and out with bandages, lint, medicines, and food, and there was an ever present sense of anguish, dread, pity, and, I fear, hatred. These are my recollections of Antietam.

The efforts of these civilians and those in many other nearby villages saved thousands of lives. The residents paid their own price, though, in nightmares and nagging memories and the loss of any innocence they might have yet possessed. No longer could they deny the nature and expense of the war they had sent their young men to fight.

McClellan Risks Nothing

George McClellan's decision was not so much whether to remain at Sharpsburg or fall back but whether to attack or not. His more belligerent officers pressed him to attack. Even a newspaper correspondent reported that the military situation at the end of the first day was "favorable for a renewal of the fight. If the plan of the battle is sound, there is every reason why McClellan should win it."

There was every reason indeed. The Federals had thirty thousand men unhurt from the fighting of the day before and another thirty thousand (the reserves) who were rested and fresh. Ten thousand more would arrive on September 18, raising his overall strength to seventy thousand, and all these men had plenty of food, ammunition, horses, and supplies.

But General McClellan was not satisfied with his advantages. He still feared a Confederate attack, and he used that fear to justify his defensive posture. "One battle lost," he wrote later, "and almost all would have been lost. Lee's army might then have marched as it pleased on Washington, Baltimore, Philadelphia, or New York."

So, on September 18, 1862, Lee with his thirty thousand men faced off McClellan with his seventy thousand men. The Young Napoleon shrank from yet another opportunity to destroy the Confederate army, and then went to work attempting to convince the world that he had done the right thing.

Little Mac Falls from Grace

Angry officials in Washington demanded that General McClellan explain his inaction, and he replied:

> A careful and anxious survey of the condition of my command, and my knowledge of the enemy's forces and position failed to impress me with any reasonable certainty of success if I renewed the attack without re-enforcing columns.

This chronic lack of "reasonable certainty" ("the slows," President Lincoln had dubbed them) would eventually cause McClellan to fall from whatever favor he had enjoyed in Washington. Lincoln and his Republican allies had wanted to relieve McClellan, a Democrat, from his command much earlier, but they did not want to alienate the Democratic majority in Congress.

The congressional elections in November, however, replaced the Democratic majority with a Republican majority, making the general's dismissal much more politically acceptable. After the elections, the Young (but rapidly aging) Napoleon would be replaced by none other than Ambrose Burnside but not before exercising his command authority one last time.

Chances Lost/Excuses Offered

The sun set on Thursday, September 18, without the carnage or decisiveness of another day's battle, and General Lee slipped his army away with its equipment, wagons, and supplies intact. On Friday McClellan pursued but without much conviction. After some bloody rearguard fighting at the Potomac River crossing, the Federal commander prematurely halted this final opportunity to strike down the Confederate army.

McClellan allowed Lee to escape into Virginia and begin rebuilding his devastated force. His men had battled the Yankee multitude to an honorable draw, so they remained in remarkably high spirits. Returning stragglers and another wave of patriotic recruits soon replenished the ranks. These eager fellows streamed out of the heartland after reading the reports that the Southern newspapers were printing about Antietam, and within weeks Lee's army was ready to take on the Federals again.

Through the manipulation of Northern newspapers, official military dispatches, and personal letters, George McClellan managed to convince the country that he had won a major victory at the Battle of Antietam. A letter to his wife reflected his impressions:

> The spectacle yesterday was the grandest I could conceive of; nothing could be more sublime. Those in whose judgment I rely tell me that I fought the battle splendidly and that it was a masterpiece of art.

Little Mac could have been pardoned for some of his bragging because everyone around him desperately wanted to believe that such a victory had been achieved. Indeed, Lee's invasion of the North had been stopped, Virginia would once again have to absorb the brunt of the warfare, and England was already backing away from supporting the Confederates.

President Lincoln meets with his chief commander, George McClellan, during a visit to the Union campsite near Sharpsburg. After the draw at Antietam, McClellan lost Lincoln's support.

The Black Man Gets His Chance

Prior to the Emancipation Proclamation, no Black men, freed or otherwise, had been allowed to fight in battle. Runaway slaves in Kansas, Louisiana, and South Carolina had been given uniforms and loosely organized into battalions, but they had served as manual laborers only.

Frederick Douglass, the most influential of all Black leaders and himself a runaway slave, had long been arguing for his people's right to bear arms in the military, not only to aid in the Northern war effort but also to improve the station of all Black persons. He said, "Once let the black man get upon his person the brass letters, U.S.; let him get an eagle on his button, and there is no power on earth which can deny that he has earned the right to citizenship."

But four generations of White people (in the North as well as the South) had never witnessed a Black man perform any tasks other than those requiring a strong back. True, Blacks had rarely been given the chance to exhibit any other qualities, but the questions arising among the White population seemed logical nonetheless. Could Blacks learn to operate artillery pieces or complete complicated maneuvers in the field? Did Blacks have the courage to stand firm under fire?

Abraham Lincoln's Emancipation Proclamation would give the Blacks the chance to answer those questions one way or the other. Using recruits who were newly freed and others who had never tasted slavery, the Federal government began forming regiments of "colored troops." It paid them less, equipped them poorly, and gave them the most dangerous assignments. But the new units proved their bravery time after time, taking losses far worse than other regiments.

By the end of the war, Black troops made up 10 percent of the Union army, 200,000 men, and they had undeniably helped to achieve the ultimate victory in the field. But the greater victory came as Frederick Douglass had predicted: Their sacrifice helped gain citizenship for all Blacks. Thus, the Battle of Antietam and subsequent issuance of the Emancipation Proclamation positively and directly affected the lives, hopes, dreams, and futures of five million Americans.

The Emancipation Proclamation allowed Blacks to fight in battle. Newly formed regiments of "colored troops" bravely fought in the Civil War and helped win citizenship for all Black Americans.

All that notwithstanding, President Lincoln knew that the battle was not as great a success as McClellan claimed. However, Lincoln had been waiting since July for a campaign that would resemble a win, and now the U.S. president made the most of this perception of military advantage. He seized the chance to issue the one document for which he said he would be best remembered: the Emancipation Proclamation.

From Darkness Comes Light

Lincoln told his advisors:

> I made a vow that if God gave us the victory in the approaching battle, I would consider it an indication of Divine Will to proceed with emancipation. God has decided this question in favor of the slaves.

He then went on to declare that as of January 1, 1863, all persons held in bondage in any rebellious state or part of a state would "be then, thenceforward, and forever free."

The response was immediate. Abolitionists declared Lincoln a saint and praised him for doing what they said the country should have done years earlier. Ralph Waldo Emerson wrote, "It makes a victory of our defeats. Our hurts are healed; the health of the nation is repaired!"

Republicans applauded the action from a political perspective because it drew radical and moderate members of their party back together. The governor of Massachusetts, a radical abolitionist, found common ground with the moderates who wanted gradual emancipation when he said, "It was a poor document" (because it did not free all the slaves) "but it was a mighty act" (because it at least freed some of them).

But Northern Democrats (such as General McClellan) who had long opposed abolition railed against the president's "radical fanaticism." Little Mac himself wrote, "At one stroke of the pen (the Emancipation Proclamation) changed our free institutions into a despotism."

An officer close to General McClellan suggested that the army would never enforce it. The officer said:

> That is not the game. The object is that neither army shall get much advantage of the other; that both shall be kept in the field till they are exhausted, when we will make a compromise and save slavery.

In time, though, most Northerners would decide that emancipation was the best policy if for no other reason than that it undermined the Southern war effort by disrupting its workforce. But more importantly, the Emancipation Proclamation transformed the war from a political struggle to reunite a country into a moral crusade to free 3,500,000 human beings. And in so doing, it turned world opinion in favor of the North and isolated the South from potential allies.

Of course, the people most affected by the Emancipation Proclamation were the slaves themselves. The following passage describes how one group took the news.

> All that night we danced and sang right out in the cold. Next morning at daybreak we all started out with blankets and clothes and pots and pans and chickens piled on our backs. We didn't care nothing about the missus (the master's wife). We was going to the Union lines!

The granddaughter of another slave wrote:

> She dropped her hoe and ran all the way to the master's house—seven miles it was—and she ran to ol' missus and looked at her real hard. Then she yelled, "I'm free! Yes, I'm free! Ain't got to work for you no more! You can't put me in your pocket now!" Gramma said that the missus started boo-hooing and threw her apron over her face and ran in the house. Gramma knew it was true then.

President Lincoln and his advisors confer prior to the signing of the Emancipation Proclamation, the historic document that abolished slavery in the United States.

Mr. Stuart's Wild Ride

Robert E. Lee wanted to punch the Federals in the gut with one last parting blow before completely calling off the Maryland campaign, so on October 9 he sent the daring J. E. B. Stuart on a reckless ride through the heart of McClellan's army. In a catch-me-if-you-can type of cavalry raid, Stuart led eighteen hundred of his best troopers through Maryland, Pennsylvania, and back through Maryland again, daring the surprised Unionists all along the way to give chase.

Some Federals did, only to find themselves caught in ambushes and driven back ingloriously. Others arrived after the Rebels had done their damage and moved on to spy, burn bridges, and disrupt communication lines elsewhere.

But both sides agreed that the greatest harm done was to Yankee pride: Both Northern and Southern newspapers had a field day with the seventy-two hour raid. Everyone took a shot at the Federals, calling them inept because 100,000 of them could not handle a mere 1,800 Rebels. The embarrassment ultimately fell at George McClellan's feet, and he, of course, did all he could to minimize it.

Facts were facts, however, and the humiliating truth was this: The Confederate cavalry had thumbed its nose at the Unionists, ridden loops around and through their huge force, and escaped back into Virginia at their leisure. Further intensifying the Yankee shame, the Rebels had returned with almost no losses of their own and could claim thirty important Yankee prisoners, twelve hundred desperately needed horses, and the satisfaction of knowing that their escapade had elevated the spirit and morale of the entire South.

Perhaps there was some redeeming value to be dredged from the grisly slaughter of September 17, 1862, and from the sacrifices of those who fought there. The reasons for the war had been clarified, an inept commander had been relieved of duty, an entire race of people had been started on its way to freedom, and the war itself suddenly stood naked and exposed.

The Battle of Antietam revealed the war's horror like a coroner pulling back his bloody sheet for a viewing, but the effects were not entirely negative. Now the soldiers realized how much killing it was going to take to see the war through to its end and just what their odds were of surviving it. Consequently, with the grim determination that makes men willing to die for a cause, they steadied their nerves, toughened their hearts, and marched on to the next terrible battle.

Appendix: Biographies of the Commanders

Ambrose Burnside (1824–1881) Union General Burnside is usually remembered for two unrelated aspects of his life: for inspiring the term *sideburns* in reference to his own mutton-chop whiskers and for being a bumbling, inefficient general. The son of a former slave owner, he graduated from West Point and fought in the Mexican War. He retired from the army after being wounded by the Apaches and set up his own rifle-making factory.

His design for the rapid-loading Burnside carbine was superb but his business skills were not. Forced to sell his invention and his factory, he returned to a career in the military. After blundering his command responsibilities at Antietam and then again at Fredericksburg, Burnside finished out the war in lower-level positions. He later worked his way into politics and served as both governor of and U.S. senator from his home state of Rhode Island.

Daniel Harvey Hill (1821–1889) Confederate General D. H. Hill would not compromise on anything. What he decided was right, he knew to be right and woe to anyone who disagreed with him. This went for his religion (hellfire-and-damnation Presbyterian) and his politics (abolitionist-be-damned Democrat). On the battlefield he took a stubborn stand on whatever ground he was assigned and stayed there until ordered to leave.

For all of that, D. H. Hill was also something of a Renaissance man. He wrote books on philosophy, taught mathematics in colleges, and held the position of university president at the war's outset. His fond remembrances of West Point and the Mexican War drew him back into the military where he rose to become one of Lee's most trusted commanders. He somehow survived the bloodshed into which he so eagerly thrust himself and finished out his life as an academician.

Joseph Hooker (1814–1879) No one ever questioned Union General Joseph Hooker's personal courage, though some wondered if it didn't come out of a bottle. In battle after battle, he drove himself and his troops aggressively, if not recklessly, trading heavy casualties for conquered objectives. The West Point graduate and Mexican War veteran had plenty of shortcomings, including alcoholism, arrogance, and an inability to get along with his fellow officers, especially those who outranked him.

After recovering from wounds received at the Battle of Antietam, Hooker commanded the entire Army of the Potomac, but his humiliating failure at Chancellorsville, Virginia, in May 1863 caused him to be transferred to Tennessee where he commanded fewer men. His drinking and quarreling earned him more and more enemies until he was finally removed entirely from field service. He suffered a paralyzing stroke just after the war and spent the remainder of his life in a wheelchair.

Thomas J. Jackson (1824–1863) This Confederate general probably looked, acted, and thought less like the typical professional soldier than any other man in either army. Instead of a swaggering stride on foot and a pompous bearing in the saddle, this fanatically religious backwoodsman suffered painful self-consciousness in the presence of others. He nearly failed his coursework at West Point but salvaged his grades with relentless and determined rote memorization before going off to Mexico where he finally discovered his only natural talent: fighting in a war.

When that war ended, he retired from the peacetime army to begin ten failed years as a professor. He wasted no time in enlisting in the Civil War and earned his nickname "Stonewall" in the very first battle (Bull Run). As if transformed from eccentricity to boldness in the face of danger, he became a legend and General Lee's "right arm." However, he lost his left arm when his own men accidentally shot him at Chancellorsville, and he died eight days later on a peaceful Sabbath as he had always hoped that he would.

Robert E. Lee (1807–1870) While at West Point, Robert E. Lee earned the nickname "the marble man" because of his seemingly perfect character, intellect, and morality. Perhaps his father, who had been a Revolutionary War hero, passed on some of those qualities to him before dying when Robert was young. Lee's skill as a military engineer (designing and building forts) enhanced his reputation. Lee was promoted from major to colonel for bravery in the Mexican War, and many considered him to be the finest officer in the entire U.S. Army.

That being the case, he was given the plum assignment of putting down John Brown's raid at Harpers Ferry, Virginia, in 1859, and as the Civil War began, Abraham Lincoln asked Lee to lead all the U.S. forces. As a Virginian, though, Lee felt compelled to turn down the job and went on as a Confederate to outmaneuver a string of Lincoln's other choices. Finally forced to surrender at Appomattox Court House, he quietly spent his last years as the president of a college, respected in the North, worshiped in the South, and renowned the world over.

James ("Old Pete") Longstreet (1821–1904) James Longstreet impressed very few people during his early years. He was the son of a farmer and would no doubt have taken over the family acreage had the land not been lost when his father died in debt. Needing a free education, he gained entrance to West Point but turned no heads there either. He spent his youth as a brooding, unambitious sort of fellow in spite of his solid performance as a junior officer in the Mexican War.

When the Civil War began, Longstreet might have contented himself with his desk job in Richmond, but the South needed every West Pointer it could get. The steady, plodding Longstreet went on to earn General Lee's affectionate nickname "my old war horse" despite his caution and preference for defense.

During the Gettysburg campaign, he was less than completely cooperative with Lee's brash efforts to launch a frontal attack against the Federals entrenched on the high ground and urged a less risky sweep around the Union flank instead. Lee proceeded with his plans and lost the tide-turning battle, but the South laid the blame for the defeat on Old Pete for not supporting his revered commander.

George B. McClellan (1826–1885) Born into the wealth and privilege of high-society Philadelphia, George McClellan grew up with few wants denied and no reason to doubt that they ever should be. By the age of fifteen, the intelligent and precocious McClellan had completed coursework at the prestigious University of Pennsylvania and become the youngest cadet to enter the U.S. Military Academy at West Point, graduating second in the class of 1846.

Young McClellan displayed excellent organizational, administrative, and drilling skills throughout the Mexican War and was promoted three times for gallantry in action, but a peacetime career as a railroad executive tended to hone his administrative rather than his combative abilities. At the outbreak of the Civil War, he gained heroic status for a few minor victories but that status diminished following his blunders at Antietam. In a rapid slide, he lost his command, his reputation, and the 1864 presidential election, forcing the excessively proud man to settle for the governorship of New Jersey.

Glossary

abolish: To do away with, in this case slavery.

artillery: Large caliber guns served by five to eight men, usually mounted on wagon wheels.

battery: A group of four to six artillery pieces and their crews.

bayonet: A long, sharp blade that can be attached to the end of a rifle for use in hand-to-hand fighting.

breastwork: Trench dug to a depth of the breast of a standing man.

brigade: A group of approximately twenty-five hundred to five thousand men, or less depending upon casualties, commanded by a brigadier (one-star) general.

cannister: A bucket of lead balls that creates a giant shotgun blast when fired by a cannon.

casualty: A killed, wounded, or missing soldier.

cavalry: Mounted soldiers usually assigned to gathering information, guarding flanks, and raiding behind enemy lines.

commissary wagon: Horse-drawn vehicle from which meals were prepared and dispensed.

communication lines: Roads, rivers, or pathways kept open between commanders and their subordinates so that they can communicate orders and reports (usually doubling as supply lines).

company: Approximately fifty to one hundred men, or less depending upon casualties, commanded by a captain.

corps: Two or more divisions, approximately fifteen to thirty thousand men, or less depending upon casualties, commanded by a major (two-star) general or a lieutenant (three-star) general.

division: Usually consisted of three brigades commanded by a major (two-star) general.

emancipation: The freeing of something, in this case the slaves in the South.

field piece: Relatively lightweight, wheeled cannon capable of rapid movement to and on the battlefield.

flank: Either side of an army's position. "To flank an enemy" means to attack around the side.

front: The closest line or area of an army facing the enemy.

infantry: Foot soldiers usually bearing shoulder arms; the backbone of any army.

minié ball: A spherical cone of leaden rifle ammunition (bullet) named for its French inventor Claude Minié; used widely during the Civil War.

musket: Originally a smoothbore shoulder arm for infantry; the improved rifled pieces were often referred to as muskets as well.

muzzle loader: A weapon whose ammunition is inserted at the "business end" of the barrel.

percussion cap: A tiny, thimblelike charge designed to spark when struck by the trigger-released hammer and ignite the full charge (powder and bullet) already rammed down into the breech of a rifle.

ramrod: A thin, metal rod used for forcing ammunition down into the breech of a muzzle-loading musket. Larger ramrods were used to load artillery pieces.

regiment: A group of five hundred to one thousand men, or less depending upon casualties, usually commanded by a colonel.

rifle: A shoulder arm whose long barrel contains internally spiraled grooves for increasing the accuracy and range of the bullet.

shell: Artillery ammunition designed to explode into many deadly pieces at or near its target, usually enemy personnel.

solid shot: The classic cannonball designed to remain intact upon impact and batter down its target, usually walls or earthworks.

teamsters: Wagon drivers in charge of a team of draft animals.

trooper: A cavalry soldier.

For Further Reading

Robert Alter, *Heroes in Blue and Gray*. Racine, WI: Whitman Publishing, 1965. Inspiring stories of the courage and sacrifice of Civil War soldiers.

Robert Athearn, *The American Heritage New Illustrated History of the United States*. Vol. 8, *The Civil War*. New York: Dell Publishing, 1963. Brief, readable overview of the war, its causes, and effects. Excellent photos and illustrations.

C. Bishop, I. Drury, and T. Gibbons, *1400 Days: The Civil War Day by Day*. New York: Gallery Books, 1990. A day-by-day look at the entire Civil War. Outstanding original maps and illustrations.

Eleanor Bishop, *Ponies, Patriots, and Powder Monkeys: A History of Children in America's Armed Forces 1776–1916*. Del Mar, CA: Bishop Press, 1982. A fascinating review of the boys (and girls) who have aided our country's military efforts over the years.

Bruce Catton, *The American Heritage Picture History of the Civil War*. New York: American Heritage/Bonanza Books, 1960. Superb compilation of narrative, pictures, and action-oriented miniaturizations of the battlefields.

William Frassanito, *Antietam: The Photographic Legacy of America's Bloodiest Day*. New York: Scribner's Sons, 1978. A unique reconstruction of the battle based upon photographs taken after the fighting.

Webb Garrison, *Civil War Trivia and Fact Book*. Nashville: Rutledge Hill Press, 1992. Fun and instructional collection of questions and answers about all facets of the Civil War.

Rod Gragg, *Civil War Quiz and Fact Book*. New York: Harper & Row, 1985. Unusual facts and tidbits about the war presented in an entertaining question-and-answer format.

Curt Johnson and Mark McLaughlin, *Civil War Battles*. New York: The Fairfax Press, 1977. Short, fact-filled accounts of the war's major battles and leaders. Helpful statistics on casualties, troop strengths, and regiments.

James McPherson, *Images of the Civil War*. New York: Gramercy Books, 1992. Dramatic and moving artwork accompanied by an insightful narrative.

Eric Weiner, *Facts America: The Civil War*. New York: Smithmark, 1992. A readily understandable retelling of the major aspects of the Civil War, including causes, strategies, weapons, equipment, and uniforms. Many excellent pictures.

Douglas Welsh, *Americans at War: The Civil War*. Greenwich, CT: Bison Books, 1982. Broad sketch of the war written in a direct, uncomplicated manner. Highlights important military developments with a wide assortment of photographs, paintings, maps, and sketches.

Works Consulted

Douglas Southall Freeman, *Lee's Lieutenants*. Vol. 2. New York: Charles Scribner's Sons, 1942. Unparalleled account of the top Confederate generals. Gripping battle histories are interwoven with biographies of the generals.

Shelby Foote, *The Civil War: A Narrative*. Vol. 1. New York: Vintage Books, 1958. Nonfiction written with a novelist's voice. Inspiring, emotional, and rich with unforgettable images. Includes much anecdotal as well as purely historical information.

A. Guernsey and H. Alden, *Harper's Pictorial History of the Civil War*. 1866. Reprint, New York: Fairfax Press, 1977. Narrative with a Union slant but interesting in that it was written so soon after the war's end. Must be read critically, however. Some of the information reported was later revised.

O. E. Hunt, ed., *The Photographic History of the Civil War*. Secaucus, NJ: The Blue & Gray Press, 1987. Five volumes originally written in 1911 (the fiftieth anniversary of the Civil War). Some factual misinformation although generally an enlightened rendering of the struggle. Excellent photographs, many of them rarely seen elsewhere.

Benson Lossing, *A History of the Civil War*. New York: War Memorial Association, 1912. Compiled directly from the official records of the War Department. One-sidedly sympathetic to the Union and overly patriotic but contains a wealth of quotations from participants. Abundant photographs and exciting color plates.

James Murfin, *The Gleam of Bayonets: The Battle of Antietam and the Maryland Campaign of 1862*. New York: Yoseloff, 1965. Once considered the most important modern work on the Battle of Antietam. Delves more deeply into the battle than any previous book. Clear explanations of major events and minor occurrences.

Allan Nevins, *The War for the Union*. Vols. 1 and 2. New York: Scribner's, 1959. Scholarly overview of the war with considerable attention paid to the political, economic, and strategic importance of the Battle of Antietam.

John Priest, *Antietam: The Soldiers' Battle*. Shippensburg, PA: White Mane Publishing, 1989. The most extensive compilation of quotations from ordinary soldiers. Tells the complete story of the battle from the perspective of the combatant.

John Schildt, *Drums Along the Antietam*. Parsons, WV: McClain Printing, 1972. Thorough, well-researched work contains enough human interest stories to prevent it from becoming too dry and analytical.

Stephan W. Sears, *Landscape Turned Red: The Battle of Antietam*. New York: Ticknor & Fields, 1983. Perhaps the most authoritative effort on the battle to date. Masterfully blends the strategic, tactical, and personal aspects of the Maryland campaign with a highly readable style.

Bell Irvin Wiley, *The Life of Billy Yank*. Indianapolis: Bobbs-Merrill, 1952. The long-standing last word concerning the everyday life of the Union soldier during the Civil War.

————, *The Life of Johnny Reb*. Indianapolis: Bobbs-Merrill, 1943. The even longer-standing last word concerning the everyday life of the Confederate soldier during the Civil War.

Index

Picture Credits

Cover photo: The Bettmann Archive

Archive Photos, 45 (bottom), 55

The Bettmann Archive, 11, 21, 33, 48

Reproduced from the Collections of the Cincinnati Historical Society, 38

Collection of the New-York Historical Society, 24

Library of Congress, 10, 12 (top), 23, 30, 35, 39, 43, 44, 45 (top), 47, 51, 52, 54, 56, 60, 61, 65, 67, 69, 70, 73, 74 (both), 77 (top), 78, 81, 82

National Archives, 9, 12 (bottom), 17 (both), 18, 29, 31, 41, 53, 63, 64, 77 (bottom)

North Wind Picture Archives, 15 (top), 84

About the Author

James P. Reger hails from a West Virginia family whose history parallels that of America's itself. One of his ancestors fought with Jeb Stuart's cavalry at Gettysburg; another with Stonewall Jackson's infantry at Antietam. A third died in a Northern prison camp. Surrounded by battlefields and other reminders of the war, Reger grew up listening to the ancestral wartime lore passed down by grandparents and great-uncles whose own parents, uncles, and cousins had endured the hardships firsthand.

He formalized his study of Civil War history at West Virginia University and went on to teach social studies, English, and special education at the secondary level. When not teaching, reenacting, or performing Civil War living history sketches for school audiences, Mr. Reger resides with his wife and young son in a coastal suburb of San Diego, California.